MW00331505

Stoicism

(Three Book Box Set)

Ryan James

© Copyright 2017 by Ryan James

All rights reserved.

The follow Book is reproduced below with the goal of providing information that is as accurate and reliable as possible. Regardless, purchasing this eBook is as consent to the fact that both the publisher and the author of this book are in no way experts on the topics discussed within and that any recommendations or suggestions that are made herein are for entertainment purposes only. Professionals should be consulted as needed prior to undertaking any of the action endorsed herein.

This declaration is deemed fair and valid by both the American Bar Association and the Committee of Publishers Association and is legally binding throughout the United States.

Furthermore, the transmission, duplication or reproduction of any of the following work including specific information will be considered an illegal act irrespective of if it is done electronically or in print. This extends to creating a secondary or tertiary copy of the work or a recorded copy and is only allowed with express written consent from the Publisher. All additional right reserved.

The information in the following pages is broadly considered to be a truthful and accurate account of facts and as such any inattention, use or misuse of the information in question by the reader will render any resulting actions solely under their purview. There are no scenarios in which the publisher or the original author of this work can be in any fashion deemed liable for any hardship or damages that may befall them after undertaking information described herein.

Additionally, the information in the following pages is intended only for informational purposes and should thus be thought of as universal. As befitting its nature, it is presented without assurance regarding its prolonged validity or interim quality. Trademarks that are mentioned are done without written consent and can in no way be considered an endorsement from the trademark holder.

Table of Contents

Introduction to the Stoic Way of Life

Stoicism Mastery

Live a Life of Virtue- Complete Guide on Stoicism

Stoicism

Introduction to the Stoic Way of Life

Introduction

Congratulations on purchasing your personal copy of *Stoicism: Introduction to the Stoic Way of Life*. Thank you for doing so.

The following chapters will discuss some of the many ways that you are able to add some of the basics of Stoicism into your daily life. The Stoic philosophy may have been one that was brought to us many years ago, but it is a very relevant philosophy that we could start to use in our daily lives. It helps us to learn how to not be so worried about the things that we can't control, such as the events and the people around us, and to just work on bettering ourselves and how we react to the situations that happen to us.

This guidebook is going to spend some time looking at the different ways that you are able to handle the modern world with the help of Stoicism. We will look at how you can make things better by changing your expectations, learning what you are able to control, and so much more. When you are ready to learn more about Stoicism and how it can work for your personal life to provide more happiness overall, make sure to read through this guidebook and see how easy and relevant Stoicism can be even in the modern world.

There are plenty of books on this subject on the market, thanks again for choosing this one! Every effort was made to ensure it is full of as much useful information as possible. Please enjoy!

Your Free Gift

As a way of saying thanks for your purchase, I wanted to offer you a free bonus E-book called *"How to Talk to Anyone: 50 Best Tips and Tricks to Build Instant Rapport"*.

Within this comprehensive guide, you will find information on:

- How to make a killer first impression
- Tips on becoming a great listener
- Using the FORM method for asking good questions
- Developing a great body language
- How to never run out of things to say
- Bonus chapters on Persuasion, Emotional Intelligence, and How to Analyze People

To grab your free bonus book just <u>tap here</u>, or go to:

<u>http://ryanjames.successpublishing.club/freebonus</u>

RYAN JAMES

HOW TO
TALK TO
ANYONE

50 Best
Tips
and Tricks to Build
Instant Rapport

Chapter 1: What is Stoicism?

Before we get into how your life should be when you want to follow stoicism it is important to understand what this school of thought is all about. When you get a chance to explore this, it is much easier to see how stoicism is able to work for your needs and you can maybe figure some of the different ways that you can make changes all on your own.

Stoicism was one of the brand new philosophical movements that happened during the Hellenistic period. This school of philosophy was founded in Athens during the early 3rd century BC, but it has been practiced through many different time periods because the ideas that come with it have practical uses even today. The philosophy of stoicism is all about asserting that virtue, like wisdom, is happiness and that a judgment needs to be based on the behavior, rather than the words. It also talks about how we are not able to rely on or control some of the external events that are going on around us, but we can control how we react and our responses to what happens.

That is just some of the basic of stoicism. There are also a few central teachings that come with it as well. The ideas are meant to remind us that the world is going to be unpredictable and getting all upset about it is just going to make us unhappy when we realize that we don't have any control over it. It helps us to realize that we can't be in control, but we can learn how to find happiness inside of ourselves and be steadfast and strong, regardless of what chaos is going on around us.

Stoics are often looking to quell that dissatisfaction that is common in most of us. But while other people are going to blame external events for this unhappiness and dissatisfaction, the Stoics understand that this comes from their impulsive dependency rather than on logic. If you want to be happy, you need to learn how to rely on yourself, and not on outside events that can constantly change and you have no control over.

Stoicism may sound confusing, but it is actually not going to concern itself with some of the other complicated theories that are out there in the world. It is more about learning how to overcome some of our emotions that are considered destructive and to learn to act when we can actually do some actions. It is not meant for a lot of endless debates. It helps us to realize what we can do to make changes in our lives, and how to just be strong and not worry when things are beyond our control.

Originally, Stoicism had three leaders: Epictetus, Marcus Aurelius, and Seneca. Despite having these three that helped to start it, there are many people throughout history who have practiced Stoicism including entrepreneurs, writers, artists, presidents, and kings. For example, it was said that King Frederick the Great would ride around with some of the works of stoicism because they could "sustain you in misfortune."

Now, stoicism is still found in our modern times. Take a look at the word "stoic" in the English language. This is a word that has a meaning that is similar to what the original stoics practiced when the religion started in that this word will refer to someone who seems to be indifferent to grief, joy, pleasure, or pain. Of course, the stoics do feel emotions and you don't have to completely give up on all of the feelings in your life in order to be a stoic.

The difference in that you need to learn how to control your emotions and find happiness from within. There are going to be events in your life that are hard, ones that don't go your way, but if you spend your time getting all worked up about the emotions that you are feeling, you are ruining your happiness, and it is mostly over things that you aren't able to control. You can enjoy the joyous occasions in your life and be happy, but you learn how to control your emotions.

While the ideas of stoicism may have started many years ago in ancient Greece, there are still many people who use this school of thought in their daily lives even in modern times. This is a great school of thought that you are able to follow if you are ready to learn how to let go of the things that are out of your control and to find your own inner happiness. In this guidebook, we will take some time to explore some of the different aspects that come with Stoicism and how you can make this work in your own life as well.

Chapter 2: Recognizing the Things That Are Under Your Control

One of the central ideas that come with Stoicism is that you need to recognize that you are not able to control everything that is going on in your life. Often we are going to get upset over things because we tried to control what was going on, but we sometimes just aren't able to do that. Stoicism looks at the idea that we are not able to have control over all the things that we should, and when we realize this and let go of the control a little bit, it becomes easier to be in control of our emotions and to think about things in a logical manner.

Now, when we take the time to think about some of our own actions, we are going to be kind of restricted on these. Mainly we are talking about the things that we do when we move or when we are talking. But the Stoics actually took this a little bit further when it came to our actions. With the Stoics, actions were also going to include our thoughts and our feelings as well. Often we think that our actions are not tied up with our emotions and our feelings, but this is due to the fact that we have not been able to master them yet.

But what doesn't count as one of these actions and what is going to be completely out of our control? According to some of the founders of Stoicism, the things that are out of our control include the state of our reputation, property, and body. For example, we can do some things in order to try and fight off an illness, but there are times when we are still going to become sick. We can work to make our property look nice and keep it protected, but there are still times when someone may come and steal our car or something else that belongs to us. We may work hard to have a good reputation and get others to like us, but there will still be times when a few people may not be that fond of us.

Even though we aren't able to control some of these things, there are very few days that are going to go by for the average person where they aren't going to experience at least a little bit of frustration in the things that they aren't able to control. Many people are going to get nervous and fret when the bus ends up being late, or they don't want to get out of bed when an investment didn't work out for them, or we are upset when a co-worker or a new acquaintance doesn't seem to like us.

But all of these things are out of our control. As long as we are living a life that is virtuous and good for us and we learn how to think in a logical manner, the rest is out of our control. When we learn how to take some steps back from these situations and we learn how to recognize that we really have very little power over what is going on in our lives, the reactions that we are giving to these situations are going to start to look a little bit silly.

When there is nothing that we are able to do about these situations, doesn't the reaction of getting mad, moping, fussing, and being angry seem a little bit silly now? But that is how most of us are going to react because we feel like we need to have this control over everything that comes near us.

And this is why this is a first step to understanding Stoic wisdom. We need to look at a situation and be able to identify when it is out of our hands and we need to treat it in the right manner. Our thoughts, our opinions, and our own personal actions are in our hands, but the way that people react to us and some of the situations that happen to us on a daily basis, are completely out of our hands and rearranging our actions to fit in with this can make a big difference in how we act and how happy we feel.

Chapter 3: Conforming Our Reality

There are so many times when we are going to try to take reality and make it conform to our own desires and expectations. Often, we are going to find that our own behaviors and attitudes are going to have some tension when compared to how the world really is. Yes, we all wish that we were able to make some changes in the world and see it the way that we would like, but this is just not reality and when we try to force reality to change, we are going to be the ones that are disappointed.

There are many times when we are going to try and change the things that are going on in reality; some of them can be pretty extreme and others are going to be pretty simple, but any of them can create some tension when you try to force reality to fit in with your ideas. We often will make plans to go on travel, for example, assuming that there isn't going to be any delays in the traffic or we may try to make supper and will assume that we are not going to burn the main ingredient. We may even head off on a hike with some friends and assume that it isn't going to rain. Yet, most of us have enough experience to know that these are situations where the exact opposite can occur.

Even though we know that things may not go our way at times, we often get frustrated when the reality didn't match up with the expectations that we had. We want everything to be perfect, we want to make supper without burning it or to get through traffic without issues, but that is not always reality. And understanding that there are things that are beyond our control will make a difference in whether there is tension in our lives or not.

The Stoics are big advocates for taking things in with a clear-eyed view. The outlook that is followed by most Stoics is going to be one that is realistic, one that isn't going to fight against all of the laws of natures or the reality that is in the world. If we try to make reality go with our own desires and our own wishes, we are going to find that we are fighting a battle that is pretty futile. The only way to fix this issue is to learn how to conform our own expectations so that they fit in with reality.

Now, this is not to say that stoicism is all about being a philosophy or powerlessness and helplessness. In fact, stoicism is all about striving to make the world a better place. We don't have to give up our personal battles or our professional goals in order to be a Stoic; we simply need to learn how to approach these goals with some expectations that are more realistic.

We can work to make things improved or to effect change, but the idea of whether we are going to be able to succeed or not is often going to be out of our hands. It is all up to you to exercise on a regular basis or learn how to eat healthier meals so that we can get fit and healthy, but this doesn't mean that we are guaranteeing that we will never become injured or ill. We can have a say in elections and vote the way that we want, but if others vote the opposite way, that is out of our hands.

The idea of stoicism is not to sit still and do nothing in life because it is all hopeless. It is about understanding that you can do your part, but sometimes you are still not able to influence and control the outcome, no matter how hard you wish it would be so.

But with Stoicism, we need to be fine with that. When we learn that we are not able to control everything that is going on in our lives, it is easier to not get upset and not let our emotions get the best of us all the time. The main point here is to avoid the pointless fight that we are doing against reality, and instead find some better ways to live right in harmony with it all the time.

Chapter 4: Understanding How Your Emotions Work

The main determinant of whether our lives are going the way that we would like or not is our emotions. You may have noticed this with some of the other people who are in your life, or maybe even with yourself. You will notice that there is a situation that is going on with a group of people, a situation that is completely out of their control, and you will see that there is a range of emotions that go on with all of them. One of the people in the group is going to feel frustrated and angry, another person may feel sad and a bit disappointed, and one may be calm and positive no matter what happens.

All of these people went through the exact same situation, but they are all reacting in a different manner to the situation that is out of their control. Those who learn how to control the things that they have no power over are the ones who are able to remain calm and collected even in the hardest times and they may have an attitude that is at least partially Stoic. On the other hand, if you take a situation, especially one that is out of your control, and let it influence your emotions, you have some work to do.

Often the emotions that we feel are ones that help us to feel like we are in control. They are about wanting to change the situation around us so that it can be different and it is a wish that things would make a change. This is why we often have some extreme emotions when it comes to being sad, upset, and angry of situations that we are not able to change.

But the easiest way to ensure that we are able to get in control of our emotions is to learn how to understand them. When we know the reason for having one of our emotional responses, sometimes that emotion is going to seem silly in that situation and it will disappear all on its own. Our emotions are very fickle and they are able to turn around in no time at all, which is why the Stoics believe that it is so important to learn how to master these emotions and think about things logically, rather than letting these volatile emotions get the best of us.

In addition, there are many times when our emotions are going to be wrong. How many times have you been angry at a friend because you thought they insulted you? You may have seethed in that anger for hours, feeling like the friend had hurt you and thinking perhaps of the things that you would do to them in retaliation. And then later you hear that the friend hadn't said the comment about you or that you had misheard what they were saying. Now you feel like a fool for your behavior and if you did retaliate, you could have some issues with that relationship at hand.

If you reacted in the scenario above, you have let your emotions get the best of you. As a Stoic, it is important to learn that you are supposed to be the one who is in control, not all of those emotions that are taking over. Once you are able to take a step back and realize that you can't be in control of everything, it becomes so much easier to think about things in a logical manner, rather than letting the emotions get the best of you.

So when you are feeling these intense emotions, such as anger or frustration or sadness, it is often because you are trying to control some things that are really beyond your power. When you recognize these emotions for what they are and learn to let them go, it is easier than ever to relax, let the emotions go, and live a life that is much happier.

Keep in mind that when you master your emotions, it does not mean that you have to live your life without any feelings at all. Stoics have just as many emotions as anyone else, the only difference is that they are able to look at these emotions objectively, decide if the emotions belong in their lives, and then decide if they are going to actually experience these emotions of if they will let them go. It is fine to feel happiness, sadness, anger and more over the term of your life, but you need to decide when you would like to let them in.

Chapter 5: Freedom of Will

By now you are probably aware that the philosophy that comes with stoicism is all about personal responsibility. It is one that is going to paint the world as one that is largely determined and there are many things that can be in your power to control, but then there are also quite a few things that can't be determined at all. We are able to make a lot of decisions in our lives and have some control, but we all must understand that there are a lot of things that are completely beyond our control and we need to be able to just let these happen and not get upset by them.

Despite all the ideas that the world is basically set and beyond our control, the philosophy that comes with stoicism can be pretty liberating. This is because while there are many things that are completely beyond our own control, we still have some control over our own inner lives. The world around us and even our own bodies are going to be subject to forces that we can't control, but we do still have free will when it comes to this rule of thought.

With the Stoics, you are going to see that the emotional responses that we have in our lives are completely our own choices. Our attitude and our reactions are going to be the same way. When it comes to our inner lives, we are the ones who are completely responsible for what happens and we get to make them what we want. Yes, there are going to be some situations that surprise us and make it so that we think our reactions should be one way and not the other, but we can determine how we react, regardless of the situation.

There are going to be some times when we react without thinking to a situation, but over time, you are going to learn how to make some changes so that we can be more in control. You are not expected to make these changes overnight, but with some good practice, they will come to you.

How free will can help us to live virtuously

Another main component that you are going to see when it comes to stoicism is that you are expected to live in a manner that is considered virtuous. Sometimes small descriptions of Stoicism are going to make it seem like it comes across as a self-focused or a self-centered philosophy, but this is really not the case at all. Yes, Stoics are going to preach that you need to have some mastery over your emotions because this helps to improve your inner lives and can make your well-being a bit better, but you are also required to be just, empathetic towards others, and kind.

The map to feeling happy is not all about just reducing how many feelings you experience that are unpleasant, but it is all about making the lives of others better as well, whether you are doing this with big gestures or some of the smaller ones with family and friends. And while some people will argue that this has nothing to do with Stoicism at all, it is really in line with some of the core themes that we have discussed so far.

One aspect that is in common for all of them is the importance of having that good inner life, of finding happiness when you have the right mindset, and how you can enjoy a calm and a pleasant disposition towards things. This does not mean that Stoics are all about being egotistical; they want to make sure that everyone is able to experience these great inner lives and they feel that when they live in a manner that is virtuous, it is possible to help out other people as well.

There are many times when you will be able to bring some virtue into your life. You need to learn how to not be egged on when there is adversity in your life, for example, and you need to be kind, generous, and willing to help out others around you.

Every culture has their own ideas of what being virtuous is going to be all about, but there are often some similarities that are going to come up when you look at the different cultures. Studying up on what it means to be virtuous in your own culture can help put you on the right path with Stoicism.

Of course, there are always going to be people who see that you are being a virtuous person, and they are going to fight against you. Remember that you should not react to this behavior, but show it some understanding instead. Often the other person is trying to fight against you not because of something you are doing, but because of their own anger and their own insecurities. When you are able to respond to them in a manner that is more virtuous and understanding, you are the one who will be in control of your own emotions, and perhaps you can show the behavior to the other person and help them through their own ordeals as well.

Remember that while you need to be in some control of your own emotions and you need to live a life that is considered virtuous, it doesn't mean that you need to live a flat and unemotional lifestyle. Stoics are kind and helpful to all kinds of people and they have no issues with being kind and compassionate. The difference is that the Stoic is able to look at the emotion that they are feeling and decide objectively whether it makes sense of the situation without it controlling them.

Chapter 6: Learn How to be Calm, Even When Adversity Strikes

When you are looking to find a Stoic, one of the defining marks that you are going to notice pretty quickly is their ability to make it through all sorts of adversity. Stoics are going to face the same challenges that the rest of us do, but they know that they need to go for it head on and that one of the greatest roadblocks for them to reach their goals is themselves. When they get in the way of success, they are never going to get ahead. On the other hand, when they move over and face the adversity without any setbacks, it is easier to see that success.

Many times we are going to feel a bit overwhelmed by all of the things that are getting in our way. We may feel like we should just give up before we even have a chance to fight off the challenge. We may feel miserable, and we let this keep us from doing some of the things that we deserve to see a change. Sometimes we even take a sour mood and let it determine if we are going to get things done throughout the day. But when we start to bring some of the Stoic philosophy into our lives, we find that we are able to remain calm no matter what kind of adversity is facing us, and we will find that it is easier to succeed.

The biggest issue that is going to be facing a lot of people who are trying to use the Stoic philosophy is that the external obstacles, which are pretty hard to face in the first place, are going to be even harder to deal with when we add in some of the internal ones that we are trying to face as well. We can fight when there is an adversity, but nothing is going to be gained when we end up going into pieces over that adversity. But when we are fighting both together, it becomes even harder to stay levelheaded.

This is why the inner tranquility is so important to helping us to deal with some of our troubles. If we are dealing with fear, sorrow, and anger, it is futile to try at all. But if you follow some of the other Stoic principles, you will find that the inner tranquility that you are looking for is going to be easier to find overall.

While we are working on this part, it is time to make sure that we kick out some of those negative emotions. These are infectious and they are some of the hardest to fight off. If we are dealing with people who are giving us these negative emotions, our frustration and anger is going to make us preoccupied and can make it harder to find that inner peace. We need to learn how to let go of the anger or the frustration that we feel with other people, because it is beyond our control, and focus on all the good energy that we can bring in.

When the troubles do come up and start to bother us, we need to learn how to not get so worked up about them. When you learn how to keep your emotions calm and collected, it is believed that you are going to greatly improve your odds of winning and you aren't going to be slipped up so easily with depression or anxiety over the issue. When you are able to do this, even if it may seem a bit hard at times, you are going to be all the happier for it.

There are always going to be times when adversity is going to find you, regardless of the philosophy that you follow. Stoics are not immune to these adversities, they have just learned to look at them in a different way and to fight to win over them, rather than saying it is all hopeless and giving up. Your adversities may be out of your control, but the way that you react to them is not and reacting with calmness and some even emotions can make it easier to face them without the stress and the anxiety that most people deal with.

Chapter 7: Learn How to Make the Best of All Situations

The Stoics understand that there are a lot of things that can go on in their lives and that they don't necessarily have complete control over it all. They are not necessarily going to have a better life than anyone else and just because of their beliefs it doesn't mean that no trouble will ever come to them. This is not reality and the Stoics know it. But rather than getting all worked up over things they can't control, the Stoics learn to take things as they come and to not get too upset about these things.

The early Stoics faced some hardships. Zeno ended up surviving a shipwreck and Epictetus was a slave that was not treated well. These founders were not living the high life and getting everything that they wanted. They faced hardships just the same as the rest of us, but the difference was that they were able to make changes to their attitudes and how they reacted to the situations rather than allowing it to control them.

There are going to be things that happen in your life. And sometimes these will be bad things, although we can hope for all the great things to happen in our life. But when you are a stoic, it is all about changing your outlook on life and thinking about it in a logical way, rather than letting our emotions dictate how we are going to behave.

When we make the best of all situations that come our way, it doesn't mean that we just need to deal with this when tragedy is around. This is also something that you can think about when life is going well so that you can enjoy all of the good situation to the fullest. It is not all about thinking things through when the bad comes, it is about enjoying all the good that comes to your life as well.

Stoics believe that there are plenty of good times in your life and since the world is full of anger, troubles, and other issues, they believe that you should enjoy the good times even more than before. When the good things happen, you are meant to enjoy it with all of the energy that you can. Every pleasant moment and moment of peace is going to be cherished. When you live according to the principles of stoicism, it means that even if you are in a sour mood, you will never let it ruin one of your days that are going well.

While many people assume that a Stoic is going to be someone who has no interest in being happy, someone who is indifferent to the many good and the bad situations that are in their lives, it is actually a roadmap that can be used for your own happiness. The Stoics are able to look at things more logically, which allows them to not get caught up in some of the bad emotions of their life. When you don't feel angry, upset, or jealous about all of the different things that are in our lives, it is easier to feel happy.

This is sometimes a hard thing for us to learn how to use. There are bad situations that are going to happen to us, and often we feel like we are the only ones dealing with the issue. We may lose our jobs at work, get stuck in traffic, have something that breaks in the house, have someone pass on and so much more. There are a million bad things that can go wrong in our lives, but it is often going to be how we deal with these bad things that will influence if we are able to get past it and start to feel better.

The Stoics do not ignore the bad stuff in their lives and they do not have better lives than the rest of us. They are going to deal with the same issues that the rest of us do, but they have learned how to control some of the emotions that they have when these bad things do occur. Instead of holding onto some of these bad things for days to come, they realize that feeling this way is just cutting into some of their happiness, into some of the good times that they could be having, and they decide that the situation is not that important any longer. They are able to control those emotions, feel better and enjoy more of the good times, rather than letting the bad times take over everything.

Imagine how that would feel. How it would feel to have something happen to you, but then get to feel free from it a short time afterward? This is something that can happen to you if you are able to work with the ideas of stoicism and you learn how to not let your emotions hold over you for a long time. No matter what goes on in our lives, we really don't want it affecting us for a long time and holding us back from our true happiness and with Stoicism, we are able to have better control over that.

We get to be in control of the emotions that are in our lives. We get to choose whether we are going to be happy, sad, upset, or excited. When we follow the Stoic philosophy, we are better able to handle the bad stuff and we can choose when we get upset (if it makes sense to the situation) or when we will let things go and hold onto our happiness.

Chapter 8: How to Use Stoicism to Make Your Life Better

We have spent some time talking about the components that come with Stoicism so far in this guidebook. But now it is time to learn how we are able to take the ideas of Stoicism in order to make our lives better. Many times because Stoicism is an ancient philosophy, many people assume that it isn't going to have any relevance in their lives today. They may find that it is something that is dry and they won't be able to use it for themselves. But while you may not have as much hardship in your life as Zeno or Epictetus, but there are still many ways that you are able to use this in your modern life.

The reality is that in this modern world, many of us still have an inner life that is out of balance. We can look at someone who seems to be all in line, with a good job and a good family, but they may feel a lot of stress and like something is not in line for them. When we look around to find the cause of all this misery, we find that it is a by-product of our modern lives. Most of the issues are going to boil down to having expectations that are inflated. Even those who seem like they already have it all in their lives can be missing things because they still want to have control over things that they can't.

Let's take a look here at some of the things that we can use the idea of stoicism for when it comes to our modern life.

Your expectations and well-being

When we think about our modern world, we see a huge culture of expectations. All of us are expecting things almost every minute of our day. First, we are going to see all of this advertising that is around us, with promises that are not going to be delivered at all. Most advertisements are not trying to just sell a product, they are trying to sell an ideal that you will supposedly reach when you use the product. You are not just buying a suit, you are buying the prestige and lifestyle that come with that suit. You are not buying a drink, you are buying fun. Of course, most of us may think that we will never fall for this kind of thing, but in reality, we all fall for it at least a bit when we make purchases.

Then there is our education and upbringing. Chances are you are like many other families and you grew up believing that you are able to do anything if you just worked on your grades and you were yourself. Often school spends more time drilling in the idea that you can do well in school and then when you are done with that, you will do well in life. And for some people, this is a reality. But there are times when you will get good grades and do well in school, and then you may fail in life or have a hard time. This is just reality. It doesn't mean that there is something wrong with you, but since we were lead to expect that if we do well in school, we will do well in life it is easy to become disappointed when things don't work out.

And then there is even a more modern threat that comes to our happiness. This is social media. How many times can we get on social media and see beautiful snapshots of the lives of others, about their vacations, their dreams, and so much more? While it is a great way to keep up with other people, it is going to make us feel inadequate, no matter what good things we have in our lives. There is always someone who has done more, or something different, than us. With social media creating expectations that we never knew we had, it is hard to feel good after spending some time on one of these sites.

When we have all of these sources creating some false expectations in our lives each day, it is no wonder that most of us are unhappy and having issues. We may feel that we have a lot of stress, depression, anxiety, and even fear and some of these are going to bring physical repercussions as well.

Because of all these modern ailments, it is even more important to bring Stoicism into our lives. It is going to help us to alleviate some of these expectations and look at them in a more logical way. We will be able to see how the social media is bothering us, how we will have to put some work into being successful (school is not always enough), and that the advertisements are not able to give the lifestyle that we think it will.

There are a number of ways that stoicism will be able to help out with your expectations and help you to have a healthier and happier lifestyle. Some of these include:

Social anxiety

Humans are social animals. We like to have the company of others and we enjoy having conversations that are meaningful to others. Despite this, we may find that we have a harder time approaching others and when we do approach them, we end up ruminating endlessly over this situation, thinking of the ways that we did things wrong. It is common for us to deal with a situational avoidance, which is that sometimes we will avoid going to a party or another situation because we don't feel like facing the people who are around us.

Social anxiety is often going to revolve around the worry of how others are going to perceive us. We worry that people will not like us, that they will think we aren't smart enough or cool enough. These worries may even get bad enough that we will stop going to social situations altogether because we aren't able to enjoy them.

One of the reasons that we are feeling this way is because we have certain expectations of the situation and we are disappointed when the reactions of others are not something that we can control. When we learn how to manage these expectations a bit, we are better able to control our emotions. The stress and the anxiety that we are feeling are going to be lower and they will disappear altogether. This can eventually help you to get over the social anxiety that you are feeling because you don't have to worry about controlling the situation so much.

Fearing death

There are very few things in the world that will scare people more than the fear of dying. And this is a huge issue that a lot of people deal with and it seems insurmountable. Because we don't understand what death is and we aren't able to control it, it is something that brings a lot of anxiety and fear to us.

But when it comes to the stoics, they look at death in a calm manner, in a manner that does not bring out anxiety. How are they able to do this?

The reason that stoics are able to feel this way is because they are able to see that they have absolutely no control over death. We are all going to die at some time, and the time that we die is out of our control so why bring in all of this anxiety and worry instead of just enjoying life and everything that we are given?

The first step for this is to start accepting our fate. In order to overcome our fear of dying, we need to remember that we are going to die at some point, and then work to live a life that is full and that is good for us. When we remember that death is just a part of our lives and we can't control it, we are more likely to try and live our current lives in the most efficient manner possible. Some stoics even focus on making their own deaths familiar to them, working to make it so that they understand and feel comfortable with their death so that they are less likely to fear what is going to happen to them in the future.

When you learn to get rid of some of your fear of death, it is much easier to relax and get some of the things that you want out of life, rather than always feeling anxious.

Achieving your goals

Many times the people that we look up to are entrepreneurs, people that are successful, have great attitudes, and are going to have one of the best luck with getting things done. There are different kinds of entrepreneurship and the stoics do favor it and when you use some of the insights that come with stoicism, it is easier to have some of that success for yourself.

One of the biggest secrets that you are going to find with entrepreneurs is that they will fail fast and they will fail often. There are very few ideas that are going to be winners in the real world and the best way to figure out which ones can win is to test them out. For those who aren't following some of the stoic ideas, though, you may find that you try out one of the ideas, it fails, and then you would throw it all away because of that one idea.

Stoicism is about persevering and never giving up. It is about understanding that you are able to make big changes in your life and do great things, but there are times when you will fail and it is out of your control. When you reach a failure, rather than letting it get you down and prevent you from trying again, you are going to look at it objectively, find out where you made some mistakes, and then move on to trying out the next idea.

When you are able to keep your emotions out of the mix, it is so much easier to keep on going and to make decisions that are logical for your own needs.

Dealing with the chaos

In our modern times, we are used to dealing with all of the chaos that is around us. We are overworked and always on the run. We deal with things that stress us out and we can't even pick up a newspaper or watch a television show without finding out that something else is wrong with the world. Stoicism is a great philosophy because it helps us to deal with all of the chaos that is around us. But here, we are going to focus on one aspect of the chaos, parenting.

Dealing with your children is not always the peaceful affair that you would like. There are long nights without a lot of sleep, children who refuse to eat, crying, tantrums, issues with behavior, lots of questions, and just a general amount of craziness. No matter how hard we work at parenting, we are always going to feel like we are coming up short at the end of the day. We may lose our patience, we may not have fed them the healthiest meal that day, we let them go out of the house without matching socks or something else that makes us feel inadequate.

You will find that in all of this chaos and lack of sleep, there is some room for the principles of stoicism. The first step is to remember that you need to live virtuously. We aren't able to bring about harmony inside of ourselves without putting that same harmony into the world. As parents, we can do this by understanding that our children are going to depend on you for their needs and that we are doing our duty when we take care of them.

Again, managing our expectations when it comes to raising our children can also be important. All of us have some kind of expectations that we hold on to tightly when it comes to our children. We hope that they grow up to be good people, but from day to day, we hope that we can get to daycare or school on time, that they will get along with others, or even if they would sit still and be quiet for ten minutes.

But when it comes to children, we learn quickly that they are not always going to do the things that we want them to. Often, they are going to do the opposite. If you hold onto these expectations too tightly, you will find that you are really going to be worn out and tired by the end of the day when your children act the way that feels best for them. You aren't able to control everything that goes on in your life, so sitting back and relaxing a bit can help out so much. When you let go of some of those expectations, you will find that your time with your kids is so much better overall.

Our expectations are often the reason that we are going to feel miserable or that our lives are not necessarily going the way that we would like. We want things to work out perfectly, to reach all of our goals, to avoid death, and to have perfect children, but all of these are beyond our own personal control. If we keep holding onto the idea of being in control, we are going to end up failing in the end. But when we use the Stoic idea of looking at things objectively and not concentrating on the things we have no control over, it becomes easier than ever to be happy and to actually enjoy life.

Chapter 9: Using the Process of Neuroplasticity

So now we are going to take the time to look at how we can add some of the thoughts of Stoicism into our lives. We need to be ready to make some of the changes that are needed in order to really see the results. Too many times we promise that we are going to make a change or we talk about what it would be like if things changed, but often we get stuck without any change in our daily lives. If you would like to be able to finally see some of that change in your life, it may be time to work with a couple of different processes to make this happen.

The first one we are going to use that will help with implementing stoicism into our daily lives is neuroplasticity. To keep this simple, this is the idea that our brains are malleable, that they can be changed rather than being static. The brain is dynamic and we are able to change the way that it functions simply by thinking or stating something.

So even though you have been in a rut for some time or you are in the same cycle of doing things day in and day out, it doesn't mean that you are not able to make some of the changes that you would like to see some great results. You just need to believe it and even state it on a regular basis. Consider what this could mean for your life. If you are able to change the way that you react to situations, people, and thoughts, you will be able to change the way that you are looking at the world.

For years we believed that the brain would become cemented and that it would be too hard to change the mold after we reached a certain age. But it turns out that even though some of the brain may feel stuck, there is always a chance to make some changes. You can use the ideas of stoicism to help you to form the brain a bit and make it into something that you really want.

When you start engaging in a brand new repeated behavior, or you are working on creating a mindset that is going to be consistent in your life, whether it is a good or a bad mindset, there are going to be brand new neural connections that are made. In fact, any time that we try out something that is new, have a new idea, or form a memory, these new neural connections are going to be formed. These little changes are what make up your brain. This is pretty good news for you because it literally means that you are the one in control of molding your brain because you can form these new connections at any time that you would like.

There are many things that you are able to do with this information. you can decide to kick an old habit that has been bothering you or take up a brand new habit. You can rewire the brain so that you are able to change the way that you react to your anxieties and your fears and so much more. You can essentially change up the brain so that it will follow the different ideas that come with stoicism.

Just holding onto the knowledge that the brain can be rewired can be one of the first steps that you need to change it for the better. You will then be able to work on rewiring it to the way that you would like.

We are going to do a little activity for the next few weeks. Remember the tenets of stoicism that we talked about in chapters 2 to 8? We are going to use those to see how we currently react to the situations in our lives. For the next eight weeks or so, we are going to take some notes on how we will react to any of the circumstances below that apply to us including:

- When we feel distraught
- When we are fighting things that we have no control about
- When we feel that we have lost control
- When we think about death in a way that is negative rather than enjoying our lives.
- When we are replaying events in our mind and wishing that we had acted in a different way or that the events had been different.
- When we are trying to rebel against our present reality.
- When we allow our fear of dying to prevent us from taking some of the risks that are appropriate for us.
- When we allow the fear of social situations to prevent us from going out and having fun or meeting new people.
- Knowing that there is something important that we should be getting done, but we decide to do absolutely nothing instead.
- Allowing some of those negative thought patterns to dictate how we are going to act.
- When we allow ourselves to not make decisions or to become flustered because of our life circumstances.
- When we refuse to think about the needs of others because we are concentrating on our own needs.
- When we want to control other people or every circumstance that is in our lives.
- When we experience helplessness.

As you can imagine, this can take up a lot of time, but just take some notes, even if it is just in your head, about how you react to these situations. This is not a time to be judgmental about yourself or to dwell on them. Just be an outside observer and notice whether the reactions are the right ones for the situation or not.

This is going to make it easier to make some changes in the way that you are living. If you are not happy about the answers or the responses that you are giving to any of the situations above, it is time to use the idea of neuroplasticity in order to make some changes. You can start to understand that you don't have control over the things that are going on in your life. You can start to make some changes to the way that you think about the things that are in your life.

Things are going to be out of our control at some points and we may feel helpless and alone when this happens. But the ideas of neuroplasticity and of stoicism can come in and help you to change some of these negative thought patterns, free up your mind from all the worry, and help you to feel so much better overall!

Chapter 10: Using Affirmations for Stoicism

Another option that you are able to use when it comes to adding in some of the ideas of stoicism into your life include affirmations. These affirmations are basically statements that you will use in order to influence, and also ultimately shape, the brain. If they are done right, you are able to use these statements in order to form some new neural connections. When you are affirming something, it means that you are going to state it as true.

Now, most of us are going to use this in the wrong manner. We will see that we make a mistake and think that we must be dumb or that no one likes us. And even though we don't think so, these negative thoughts are forming new neural pathways that could lead us to a horrible way of thinking about the life that we have.

If you are struggling with fear or some of these other negative thoughts, it is most likely that you are telling yourself affirmations that will keep you in this spot. When you struggle with something and tell yourself that you will never be able to accomplish it, you are most likely never going to succeed. The more that you believe that something is true, especially when it regards the things that you can do or can't do, the more often it is going to become true.

Usually. this is in relations to some things that can be a little silly. For example, you may be able to lead yourself to believe that you are not good in social situations and that no one wants to talk to you, so you avoid going to social situations. In reality, you are probably just fine in these situations, but since you have convinced yourself otherwise, you are going to end up with some issues with fighting these thoughts.

It is fine to have some realization that you aren't able to do everything that you would like in life. Not everyone can fly a plane or lift 300 pounds. But when you let the irrational fears get in the way, you are really limiting yourself in ways that really aren't necessary.

Remember that your brain is going to be malleable and it can be influenced by the thoughts that we are having. This means that if we choose positive affirmations, rather than the negative ones that have been influencing us for a long time, we may start to feel so much better.

Let's take a look at the idea of confidence. If we struggle with confidence, we would use the idea of affirmations in order to tell ourselves that we are confident. This may seem a bit like we are trying to deceive ourselves, but this is because we somewhere along the line fell into the lie that we aren't confident. Affirmations let us learn the truth by shaking things up a bit, and helping us to act in the right way. When you use affirmations in the right way, such as telling yourself that you are confident, you are going to be able to add some more confidence to your life, regardless of what those negative thoughts were saying in the past.

Another thing to consider is whether you are confident in certain situations. Some people are confident around some of their friends and their family members, but then when they get into a new social situation, they are going to be shy and worried. Using the affirmations to help you to get further with the confidence and believing in yourself that you are confident will help to bring that part of your personality out no matter where you are.

The hard part about these affirmations is that many of us are going to struggle with the negative thought patterns. We believe these negative thoughts because we think that is who we really are. In reality, we can be so much more, we just need to take a detached look, a look without all the emotions involved, and then see how much better our lives can be when we believe in ourselves, rather than believing in all the lies.

You are able to start right away with creating your own affirmations that will be relevant to your current situation. Not all of us are suffering from issues of feeling unconfident, but maybe we aren't proud of our past actions or about our body image. This is one of the great things about affirmations, though; we are able to change them to make them work for ourselves.

When you pick out the affirmations that you would like to use, make sure that you say them at least twice a day, once when you get up in the morning and once when you are ready to go to bed. Don't rush through them either because this can make you feel like they are false and it is harder to feel like they matter to you. If you are stuck on which affirmations you should be using, check out the site freeaffirmations.org and see what options they have available for you.

When you first get started with affirmations, remember that it is sometimes going to feel a little bit strange. You have come to believe all the falsehoods that are given to you through these negative thoughts so it is sometimes hard to believe all of the positive things that are out there about you. But with some practice, and saying the affirmations that you choose with pride, you will be able to see results and soon your negative thoughts will be replaced with ones that are more positive in no time!

Chapter 11: Implementing the Stoic Philosophy into Your Life

We have taken quite a bit of time to talk about the Stoic philosophy and what it can mean inside of your life. Here we are going to take some time to go through each of the themes that come with stoicism and discuss how you are able to implement them into your own life with the help of affirmations, neuroplasticity, and even with visualization. For each of them, we are going to make it a little easier by discussing the behavior that is opposite as what you should do to make it stoic, what would be the right stoic action, and then the steps that you can take to make them change. Let's take a look at how this is going to work:

Recognizing what is under your control

The un-stoic: becoming angry, frustrated, and anxious at another person, or at a situation, that you are not able to control. For example, if you are getting a ride and the car gets a flat tire and you are late for a meeting, this is not something that you are really able to control. But many people will get all upset about these things.

The stoic: you should look at this situation and realize that it is something that is completely beyond your control. There is nothing that you can do about these and getting upset is not going to get you anywhere. You should stay calm, and think logically the best way to solve the situation.

The action plan: know that when something happens, you will not need to react in anger and frustration. If you are used to getting frustrated easily, go through your affirmations where you can make statements about being in control of how you react to the situations so that you can react in a manner that is completely relaxed.

Conform to reality

The un-stoic: you will become outraged and feel hopeless when you find that the reality that is around you is not aligned with what you want it to be. For example, if you planned a wedding for a long time and it rains, you may get upset because the day didn't turn out the way that you wanted.

Stoic: you will need to conform to the reality that is happening in the situation, and this may mean that you will need to adapt in some cases.

The action plan: you can stop and envision yourself as accepting the reality that is there. Focus on the things that you are able to change, such as making a contingency plan in case it does rain, and changing the way that you are going to react to the different situations.

Understanding your emotions

The un-stoic: here you are going to just let your emotions do what they want. You are going to let them run wild when you have something happen and you are not going to keep them in check. It is always best to keep them under your own control rather than letting them control you.

The stoic: learning how to not allow some of the bad emotions gain a foothold inside of your mind. There are going to be times when your ego is threatened or when something goes wrong. Learning how to keep the emotions in check is very stoic.

The action: imagine how it feels when you are being insulted and then how it would feel to not stew for hours at a time. Imagine how it may feel to be assertive at the moment, but when it is truly in your past, you will want to just imagine letting it go.

Freedom of will

The un-stoic: this is when you will experience some inner turmoil when things are not going the way that we would like around us. This can also include telling ourselves that we are a certain way because of the opinions of some others. Often this is going to have nothing to do with reality.

The stoic: no matter what is going on around us, we are able to choose how we run our inner lives. That is one of the few things that we can control.

The action: to start this, we need to visualize ourselves being at complete peace, even if there is a lot of chaos all around you. You can also create affirmations concerning how to maintain a healthy inner life, no matter what is going on around you.

Live in a virtuous way

The un-stoic: this is when you are going to focus only on yourself as well as your selfish needs in order to feel happy. But in reality, we are not able to feel happy unless we take away from the selfish behaviors that we are dealing with and start to help out people.

The stoic: to realize what is true happiness, we need to do well by some others, not just for ourselves.

The action: a good way to make sure that you are living in a manner that is virtuous, you need to learn how to be an instrument for being good inside your community. You can visualize how it will be to assist others and how much satisfaction you are going to be able to get from this.

Learn how to be calm even when adversity is around

The un-stoic: when we face adversity, we will often become pessimistic, lazy, morose, angry, and even hopeless. This makes it hard to stand up to adversity and learn how to make the best of it.

The stoic: when you practice stoicism, you will realize that spending all your time angry or depressed over something that you are not able to control, it is only going to detract from living a life that is happy and healthy for you. You can only be happy if you are able to look at things objectively and not feel overwhelmed or let these feelings take over your life.

The action: take some time to write down a few adverse events that could take place in your life. then imagine how you would normally react to them. Then change the way that you look at things and imagine how you would feel if you reacted with hope, purpose, and accepted reality.

Making the best of all situations

The un-stoic: this is when we are not going to be able to enjoy the pleasurable circumstances that are going on in our lives because of something that happened during the past. Or we will spend so much time ruminating on the negative aspects of a past experience, or one that just happened, that we end up missing out on an opportunity to have positive things in our life.

The stoic: the stoic is going to learn how to make the best of all the situations that are around you. This is when you will realize that maybe there were some bad things that have happened in the past, but you decide that you are not going to let them change how much you enjoy the preset moment. You can realize that the bad stuff happened, but you are not able to change them and so you will make the best of them so that you don't miss out on happiness later on.

The action: to help with this, envision yourself responding to both the undesirable and the desirable situations that come up in your mind. You are going to meet both of these situations with an open mind, changing only what you have some control over and learning how to accept what reality is. Make sure that you are envisioning yourself without letting the anger or the frustration blind you to some of the good things that are going on around you.

As you can see, it can be pretty easy for you to adopt some of the Stoic philosophies into your daily life. many people assume that the Stoic philosophy is too old for them to follow, something that comes from ancient times and is not for them at all. But in reality, in these chaotic and trying times, we need the ideas of stoicism more than ever. When we learn how to add stoicism into our daily lives, it is easier to live a life that is happy, rather than one that is chaotic and controlled by our emotions.

Conclusion

Thank for making it through to the end of *Stoicism: Introduction to the Stoic Way of Life.* I hope it was informative and able to provide you with all of the tools you need to achieve your goals.

The next step is to start implementing some of the topics that we discussed in this guidebook into your daily life. The principles of Stoicism are pretty easy to follow, but most of the time we misunderstand them because we assume that Stoicism is too hard to work on or that it is an ancient idea that has nothing to do with what we are living with today. But in reality, people in the modern world need Stoicism more than ever in order to face adversity, get through the hard parts, and start to feel more comfortable and happy with who they are.

This guidebook took some time to talk about Stoicism and some of the main components that go with it. We learned how to understand our emotions so that we can be in control of them, rather than letting them control us, how to make the best of every situation, how to stay calm, and even learning what things are in your control and which things are not. When you combine all of these together, it becomes easier to enjoy life and get more out of what you have.

When you are ready to start using Stoicism in your own life and see some of the happiness that you are looking for, make sure to read through this guidebook and learn as much as possible about how Stoicism can work for you.

To your success.

Stoicism Mastery

Mastering the Stoic Way of Life

© Copyright 2017 by Ryan James

All rights reserved.

The following Book is reproduced below with the goal of providing information that is as accurate and as reliable as possible. Regardless, purchasing this Book can be seen as consent to the fact that both the publisher and the author of this book are in no way experts on the topics discussed within, and that any recommendations or suggestions made herein are for entertainment purposes only. Professionals should be consulted as needed before undertaking any of the action endorsed herein.

This declaration is deemed fair and valid by both the American Bar Association and the Committee of Publishers Association and is legally binding throughout the United States.

Furthermore, the transmission, duplication or reproduction of any of the following work, including precise information, will be considered an illegal act, irrespective whether it is done electronically or in print. The legality extends to creating a secondary or tertiary copy of the work or a recorded copy and is only allowed with express written consent of the Publisher. All additional rights are reserved.

The information in the following pages is broadly considered to be a truthful and accurate account of facts, and as such any inattention, use or misuse of the information in question by the reader will render any resulting actions solely under their purview. There are no scenarios in which the publisher or the original author of this work can be in any fashion deemed liable for any hardship or damages that may befall them after undertaking information described herein.

Additionally, the information found on the following pages is intended for informational purposes only and should thus be considered, universal. As befitting its nature, the information presented is without assurance regarding its continued validity or interim quality. Trademarks that mentioned are done without written consent and can in no way be considered an endorsement from the trademark holder.

Introduction

Congratulations on purchasing your personal copy of *Stoicism Mastery: Mastering the Stoic Way of Life*. Thank you for doing so.

The following chapters will discuss some of the many ways that you are able to add stoicism into your own personal life. Many people mistakenly believe that you can only practice stoicism if you are from ancient Greece or if you make some major changes to your current life. But in reality, stoicism is still as relevant as ever and with some simple additions and modifications to the life that you already have, you are able to become a Stoic.

This guidebook is going to talk about simple ways to take the Stoic philosophies and learn how to make them a part of your habits. We are going to discuss how sharing empathy with others, giving up control of the events that go on around you, living virtuously, and even how to contribute willingly to your society ad community will be able to help you live a truly Stoic life.

When you are ready to bring some of the ideas of stoicism into your daily life without having to change up everything about your life, read through this guidebook and learn just how stoicism, and its simple philosophies, will be able to make such a difference in your life.

There are plenty of books on this subject on the market, thanks again for choosing this one! Every effort was made to ensure it is full of as much useful information as possible. Please enjoy!

Chapter 1: What is Stoicism?

Stoicism is an interesting idea from ancient times that has really translated over to modern times. It came out during a time of great turmoil in ancient times, a time when emotions could get out of hand and life was not a predictable thing like before. The tenets that come with Stoicism often work well with times that are tough, times of misunderstanding and conflict, which is why it can sometimes work so well in our modern times.

The ideas behind Stoicism help you to find true happiness. This philosophy is meant to put you in control of your emotions, allowing you to look at the situation logically, rather than letting your emotions get out of control and determine how you react, sometimes making you to react in ways that you are ashamed of later on. In addition, you will be able to understand how others react in some cases, keeping your relationships strong while also working with helping out others.

The history of Stoicism

Before we are able to look at how to get started with Stoicism, we need to have a bit of background about Stoicism. Stoicism is a philosophy that was founded by Zeno of Citium around the 3rd century BC. The philosophy asserts that the follower needs to have virtues, like wisdom, in order to find happiness and that any judgment needs to be based on the behavior of the other person, rather than on their words. Stoicism often talks about how we are not the ones in control of, and that we can't rely on, the external events that go on around us. But we can control how we respond to these events.

Stoicism is a pretty simple philosophy, but in many cases, it can be hard to stick with. It works to remind us that the world is unpredictable and that our moment in life is pretty brief. It works to teach us how to be strong and steadfast and that to find true happiness with our short time on this earth, we need to be able to control ourselves.

It also recognizes that many people are unhappy in life, but the source of this dissatisfaction is not in having too little money or not having enough stuff, it is with our dependency on our emotions and acting out right away, rather than using logic.

One of the nice things that you can find with Stoicism is that it doesn't spend time with complicated theories that try to explain the world. Rather, it spends its time trying to help us to fight and overcome some of our own destructive emotions and how to act when actions can be taken. The principles of Stoicism are all about action, not debating all of the time.

There are three principal people who are considered leaders of the ideas of Stoicism. Marcus Aurelius was one of the most powerful people in the world at that time as the Emperor of the Roman Empire at that time, and yet he sat down every day to write out some notes on the topics of compassion, humility, and restraint. Then there was Epictetus, who spent much time as a slave and then endured in order to begin his own school in which he was about to teach some of the greatest minds in Rome. And then there was Seneca, who was turned on by Nero and asked to commit suicide, was then able to think only of comforting his friends and his wife.

But while those three are considered the leaders of Stoicism, there are many others who have practiced it throughout the ages, including entrepreneurs, writers, artists, kings, and presidents. Both modern, as well as historical, men, are able to show Stoicism as their way of life.

For example, the founding fathers spent time being inspired by the ideas of Stoicism. It is said that George Washington learned about Stoicism at the age of 17 by his neighbors and then later he put on plays, including one about Cato, to help inspire his men at Valley Forge. Thomas Jefferson kept Seneca right beside him on his death bed. Adam Smith, an economist, write out theories of interconnectedness, or capitalism, and much of his ideas where influenced by the ideas of Stoicism.

These are just a few examples of how Stoicism has expanded to mean much more than just an ancient philosophy. It is one that has helped countless people to overcome their dissatisfaction in the world and to find happiness. While it may have occurred in ancient times, people of today will be able to find it useful as well.

Stoicism will differ compared to many of the existing philosophies in one main sense, it is more about action and putting the ideas to work, rather than just talking about them all of the time. If you learn how to control your emotions, learn how to control the things that you can and give up on those that you can't, and learn how to think about things logically, you are able to live the Stoic way of life and you will see a huge increase in your happiness.

Some of the basic ideas of the stoics

The Stoic ideas are great to use in order to increase the happiness you have in your life, regardless of what is going on in the outside world. Some of the basic ideas that are found with the stoics include:

- The key to living successfully and feeling happy, is to find freedom from the violent emotions. You are still able to enjoy emotions like joy and happiness, but you will be able to think about things logically and pick the emotions that are right for the situation.
- The key to get freedom from these violent feelings is to be virtuous, regardless of what others may think about you.
- The key to living a life that is virtuous is to live in a manner that is consistent with nature.
- The things that most people call good, such as a good reputation, possessions, health, and life can often be in accordance of our nature, but we shouldn't always be running around for more things.
- These things are not always in accord with our nature because sometimes they can be purchased or preserved at the expense of your virtue and your integrity.
- Successful living and virtue may not be inborn in all people, but with a deliberate choice and continuous attention you are able to figure out what is inside of your power and what is not.

The idea of Stoicism is one that is all about your happiness and enjoying life. You learn that it is not all about the materialistic things, it is about living a good life, one where you are slow to anger because you understand why others react the way that they do and where you are willing to help out other people. It is one where you are able to look at your emotions and determine if they are really the ones that will help you to be happy in that situation. Many people think that the Stoics are indifferent to everything in life, that they don't care about what is going on around them, but this is not true; they simply understand that not everything needs to be reacted to in anger or in retaliation all of the time.

Many people believe that Stoicism is an ancient thought system, one that they shouldn't follow or worry about at all because it is so old and can't relate to them. But in our modern times when emotions and materialism is all over the place, it is good to have a philosophy like Stoicism around to help us enjoy our lives and to focus on things that really matter.

Chapter 2: Practicing Gratitude in Our Lives

There are actually quite a few different ways that you can bring Stoicism into your daily life. Many times when we are thinking about how to get started on some of the ancient philosophies, we assume that we need to sit in a room and discuss and debate for a long time with other people who have spent years learning about this particular philosophy. But Stoicism has always been more about doing things, more about the common person, and learning how to implement this into your daily life can make a big difference in the amount of happiness and contentment that you can feel.

One of the first steps that we can take is to learn how to show gratitude. There are so many things that we can be grateful for in our lives, not only the big stuff but also some of the little stuff as well. Too many times we are waiting around, hoping for something big and marvelous to happen in our lives, and when that never comes to fruition, we find that it is almost impossible to feel happy in our lives.

But if we learned how to turn things around and be happy for the little things that are there, for that warm cup of coffee in the morning, that nice nap that we got to take, and so much more, it is easier to feel a little bit more happiness with the life that we are given.

When you read the first book of meditations from Marcus Aurelius, you will notice that there are some thanks that are placed in there. He spends time thanking his grandfather for teaching him some of the actions that he should use in his life such as being modest, candid and even tempered He then thanks his father for helping him to be calm and frugal and his mother for being generous. He goes on to all the different people who taught him lessons to get him where he is each day. If one of the main founders of Stoicism is able to do this, shouldn't we also spend some time each day being grateful for the things and the people who are around us?

There are several different modern techniques that you are able to use that will help you to stick with the principles of stoicism, but one of the most common ones is known as the gratitude journal. These are pretty simple things for you to keep, but in order to make sure that they are stoic and will help you through this path, you need to remember that there are a few key points that will help you out.

Some of the ways that you will be able to turn this journal into something that you enjoy using includes:

- Choose the medium that you would like to use for your journal. If you like to slow down and feel a deeper connection with the words you write, then a traditional journal is one of the best. If you like to have some instant feedback for your work, then typing on a tablet or your laptop will be fine as well. If you have a hard copy of the journal, you can consider decorating the journal to help it feel happier or to use it as a way to feel more grateful for the things in your life.
- Attach pictures: you don't have to spend the whole time writing out what you feel thankful for in order to get these to work out well. You can find some pictures that make you feel happy and place them on the cover and in random spots of the journal so that you can be reminded of the things that make you happy and grateful as you go along.

- Draw some pictures: if you are better at drawing things rather than writing them out, consider depicting some of your positive emotions as well as the other things that you feel grateful for in pictures, rather than in words.
- Write out some inspirational quotes: these may seem a little bit silly when you are first getting started, but go through and write out some different quotes on the margins that you are able to look over any time you are feeling down and need a big boost.
- Write about the special times: you are the one who is in control of what you would like to write out in the gratitude journal, but why not remember some of those special occasions. If you take the time to write them down right after they are done, you will be able to hold onto those feelings as you do the writing, and those can be a lot of fun to read back through later on, especially when you need a little bit of a boost.

When you decide to get started with a gratitude journal, you will need to remember that it is always important to be consistent with your journaling sessions. This is not something that you write down a few things in one day and then never touch for a year or more. It is best if you are able to write something down in the journal on each day. The good news is that you can write whatever you would like in this journal, there are no rules. If you only have five minutes, write down a few things that you are grateful for on that day and then move on.

Then on the days when you have a little more time, or your day was a bit tougher to get things done, spend some more time writing down the feelings and remembering all the things that you were grateful for.

What you write down is not always the most important part. The part that you should really be watching for is that you keep it consistent and you keep up with the work. So pick out a time each day that you will be able to sit down and devote at least five minutes to writing down something in the journal. A lot of people like to do this right at the end of the day so that they can share the wide range of things that they are feeling thankful for. Another option is to write out some of the things that you are grateful for right away in the morning, allowing you to have a positive start to any day.

To get started on this journal, especially if you are a bit nervous and not sure what you should be writing about, open it up and write down at least five things that you are grateful for. Each day you will write down some amount of things that you are grateful for, you can pick how many you will need to meet. This is going to force you to look at things in a slightly different light. Rather than focusing on all of the bad stuff that happened at work that day, you can turn it around and be grateful that you have a good job and that you are able to support your family with it.

In the beginning, it is going to be kind of hard to come up with the things that you are grateful for. Too many times we focus on the bad stuff and not on the stuff that really matters. That is just what we are used to. But we need to learn how to turn some of this negative stuff around and start feeling more positive, and then it will become easier to see that we have quite a few positive things to look forward to in our lives.

In addition, when you are writing out this journal, you need to learn how to be specific. You are going to find that it is hard to list out the things that you are grateful for in the beginning and sometimes it is tempting to just get the whole process over with and list out some generic things. For example, you may be thankful for your health, but you need to get a bit more specific than that. Say why you are thankful for your health or what in particular makes you thankful for the health that you have.

And always remember that this is an exercise in being positive and upbeat. One of the ideas of stoicism is to turn around the focus of different events and make them into something that is all our own. We are not able to control the events that happen around us, but we are able to control the way that we look at the events and this gratitude journal is going to help us to do that. There are many times when we are going to have tough days or things aren't going our way, but with the help of this gratitude journal, we may be able to focus our attention in a different way.

Of course, using the gratitude journal is just one of the things that you can do in order to bring more of this appreciation into your life. Giving compliments to others you see, even if it is something small like their new haircut or a new pair of shoes that they are wearing. Volunteering with others to make the community a better place is often seen as a way to show gratitude.

Some people like to show gratitude in another way, such as with voluntary discomfort. This is when the person is going to place themselves into a situation that is not very comfortable for them and they will endure it. This does not need to be something that gives you a lot of pain, but it will be a bit uncomfortable. Doing something like a day or two fast, giving up some sugar in your food, or taking cold showers can all count. This is not seen as much in modern times, but it was a pretty common practice with many of the ancient stoics.

When you do some of these different actions, you are learning how to be grateful for all of the different aspects of your life. It is not all about just showing appreciation for the good things in your life, though, it is also about showing some of the appreciation for some of the bad things that are in your life as well. When you learn to appreciate everything that is going on in your life, the good and the bad, you are going to live a happier and more rewarding life overall.

Chapter 3: How to Accept Our Faults and Nurture Our Minds

Now we are going to move on to the second set of things that we should do to improve our lives and live like the Stoics did. In this part, we are going to learn how to accept all faults. We need to be able to accept the faults that we see in others because we are not perfect either and we have some faults of our own. We also need to learn how to nurture our minds in a way that will help us to be independent, rather than being slaves to some of our selfish passions.

First, we are going to look at the idea of accepting faults. With the Stoics, we realize that all of us have faults. We need to have some empathy for the others that are around us because we have no idea what is going on with them. Yes, there are times when they may be mean to us, or they may not be around as much as we want, or there is something else that they are doing that for some reason, we don't approve of. But outside of the few things that they show us, we really have no idea what is going on with these people. Until we spend some time in their shoes, it becomes hard to really get the full results that we want in understanding what they are going through.

If we don't have empathy, we are going to be quick to judge the others who are around us. Empathy is something that should be taught to us by the other people in our lives, including siblings, grandparents, parents, and other people around us. But despite having this taught to us, many times we are going to decide to not take this into our hearts.

Sometimes we ignore the lessons because we are too busy in life. We get stuck trying to keep up with all of the things that are going on in life around us, and we find that we start to judge, not because we want to be mean and selfish, but because we are so busy trying to get everything done and we don't even think about it. Other times we are going to be more worried about what makes us happy or wanting to feel like we are the most important person ever that empathy doesn't even come into the mix.

There is a time in all of our lives that we are going to miss out on some of the empathy that we should be giving to other people. Sometimes we are going to do it on purpose and sometimes it is because we are so busy with our lives that we don't take a step back to realize what we are doing. Stoicism asks us to be empathetic to the others around us and to learn how to relate to what they are saying or doing at the time. This requires us to step away from our emotions and to think about things logically, a task that can be hard, but it is a cornerstone found with stoicism.

Learn how to become more empathetic

Many people believe that they already know how to be empathetic and how to show it, but when they need to define what this means, they are often going to feel like they are at a loss. Empathy is basically your ability to understand why someone is acting or feeling the way that they do. If you are empathetic, you will see someone who is being mean and angry at you, and understand that they are only acting this way because they had a bad day or they just got some terrible news, not because it has anything to do with you. If you see someone who is crying, you may understand that something bad happened to them and you should be there to comfort them.

This can be hard for some people to get down because they need to let their emotions go. When someone comes up and is mean to you and yelling at you, it is much easier to get offended and start yelling right back at the other person. But this is just going to elevate the situation and can make both of you feel miserable in the long run. Understanding where the other person is coming from and trying to help, or at least just letting them blow off their steam without a response from you, can help to make the situation easier.

Your ability to be able to empathize with others around you is going to be related to how well you are able to empathize with yourself. When you are able to understand your emotions and how you can react to various situations, it is easier to project those feelings onto another person who may be feeling that same way. So if you would like to learn how to be more empathetic to others, you will need to be able to understand how your reactions work as well.

There are so many benefits that come with learning how to be more empathetic. First, it helps to free you from the issues of being attached to your emotions all of the time. Remember that a Stoic is someone who learns how to think about things logically with the head rather than with their emotions. Plus, it can make it much easier to help out the others who are in your life because you learn how to understand what they are feeling and to be there when they need it most.

Living in the moment

In addition, it is important for us to start learning how to live in the moment. If we are too busy living in the past or worrying about what is going to happen to us in the future, we are basically wasting a lot of great opportunities in our lives. There are a few ways that you are able to do this including:

- Don't focus too much on the present: this may seem like it is going against what we just said, but if you try too hard, you are going to miss out on some of the great things that are going on. Just sit back and relax a little bit and enjoy the life that you are living. This doesn't have to be hard, just take a deep breath and go through life the way that you always dreamed.

- Don't always focus on the future: worrying about the future is seen as a waste when it comes to the ideas of stoicism. There is nothing that you are able to do to control the future; it is going to come whether you are ready for it or not. You can make some plans and have some dreams for what you would like to have happened in the future, but if you are constantly worrying about it and letting the ideas of the future keep you up at night, you are already going to run into a lot of issues in the long run. Learn how to just let things come as they will and you can get rid of a lot of that anxiety that is going to take over your life.

When you learn to just enjoy life as it comes, without concentrating on it too hard or worrying about what is going to happen in the future when it is all out of your control, you will find that it is much easier to relax and get some good results with the help of stoicism.

Chapter 4: Practicing Mindfulness in Your Life

The next topic that we are going to look at is mindfulness. Too many times in our lives we are going to run around, in such a hurry to get things done that we end up missing out on the little joys that are in our lives. We don't notice the smells that are around us, some of the nice noises that follow us, or any of the other things that are so important to making our lives feel amazing. There is some charm that is found in the ever day things, but we need to be able to slow down and notice them first.

If you would like to become more stoic, you need to learn how to get some more of this mindfulness into your life. This doesn't need to be something special and you won't even need to go out and get some new stuff to place in your home to make this happen, but you will need to make this a part of your routine and do some practice in order to get some of the results that you are looking for with mindfulness.

To start, you need to learn to observe the present moment. Stop whatever you are doing and just be mindful of what is going on in the world around you. You are going to pay attention to that activity. Even if it is something as simple as washing the dishes, being present in the moment, noticing the dish in your hand, the feel of the water when you grab another dish, and how they feel when they are all clean, can all help to bring more to your session of mindfulness. You would be surprised at how amazing it can be to bring some more mindfulness into your life when you take things slowly and learn how to make them into things that are fantastic.

The next thing that you can work on with mindfulness is to let some of the judgment in the world roll right off of you. If you are looking for something or someone and you start to feel like you are going to judge it, take a little mental note about that and let it pass before returning to the present moment. There are going to be times when you are practicing mindfulness when your mind is going to want to wander off. We are so used to having our minds be in a million places at once, that training the brain to be on just one action is going to take time.

But the beautiful thing about mindfulness is that while you may get distracted at times, you should be able to return back to the present moment when it is all done. You are going to be able to use it in order to really understand what is going on in your daily life, what is so amazing about the things that are going on around you, but it takes some practice with mindfulness.

Remember that during this process, you need to learn how to be a bit kinder to yourself. Your mind is going to wander; you have been training it for years how to deal with more than one topic at a time so you can't expect it to give up on that in just one day and focus on the one topic that you would like. So when your thoughts start to wander off to other things that are not on topic, don't judge yourself. Just learn to gently bring yourself back to the present and bring the mindfulness all back. This should be an experience that is all about being stress-free and making you happy so keep the judgment out and enjoy what is going on.

How to be more mindful

Being mindful is one of the best things that you can do in your life. If you are not able to sit back and learn how to bring some mindfulness into your day, you are really missing out on the little things in life. The big events can be nice, but if you are focusing all of your energy on those, you are going to give them more control over your life than you should. On the other hand, working with the little things, and appreciating all the things that you have in life can help you to be more stoic. Some of the steps that you can take to add in more mindfulness into your day include:

- Use it during routine activities: take some time to bring more awareness to the daily activities that you do, especially the ones that are usually on autopilot. Start with brushing your teeth and seeing how it actually works. Feel the toothpaste on your tongue and the movement of the toothbrush as you get those teeth to look nice.

- Practice it right when you get up: this is going to help set the tone for the rest of your day. You may find that you will need to take in some coffee or some tea to help you wake up, but spend a few minutes in the morning just sitting and thinking about your day and how great all of the things in your life before you turn on the television or checking your email.

- Allow your mind some time to wander: many times we try to make the mind stay on task for too long, but our brains like to wander and think of different things. While there are plenty of times when you would like to keep the mind on the topic, it is still a good idea to spend a few minutes a couple of times a day to just let the mind wander a bit.

- Keep things short: your brain is going to respond so much better when it can get some small bursts of mindfulness throughout the day, rather than trying to do it for an hour or more each day. A few minutes is often a good amount of time to get started and you will be able to increase it later on if needed.

- Use mindfulness when you are waiting: while we are often running around and trying to get so much stuff done during the day. But there are times when we are going to have to wait. We may wait for an appointment, wait for our turn in line, wait in traffic and so much more. But while you may feel that these are a nuisance, you can turn this over into a productive time for your meditation. You can bring your attention over to your breath and then focus on that breathing for a few moments, and nothing else. This can make the waiting so much more interesting.
- Pick your prompt: sometimes you need a cue in order to help you to get into the idea of being mindful. You can choose some kind of cue that you would come across on a regular basis and use this in order to shift the brain over to a mode that is more mindful. For example, you can use the act of drinking tea as your cue to be mindful for a few minutes before proceeding.
- Learn how to meditate: often mindfulness and meditation goes together. Often a few minutes of meditation each day will be able to help you to calm down and feel ready to appreciate the little things that are in your life. a fifteen-minute session once or twice a day can help you to feel calmer and can make mindfulness a bit easier in the long run.

Spending time on mindfulness should be one of your top priorities when it comes to working on stoicism. It is going to help you to experience things in your life in a whole new way, without making you get too attached to the different things and emotions that are trying to control you. Work on this for some time, and be gentle without the judgment, and you will find that it can be easy to appreciate the little things in your life, rather than letting everything control you.

Watching your actions

Another thing that the founders and leaders of Stoicism practiced that goes along with mindfulness is to watch out for the actions that you are performing. It is important to always behave as if someone is watching you. This is advice that we are given as children, but often we tend to forget it as we get a bit older. Over the years, we start to talk about people behind their backs, act out of line, and do things that we should be embarrassed by when we think that no one else is going to notice.

These behaviors are bad for us and it is all going to catch back up with us later on. Even though you believe that no one is watching your actions, it is going to come back and haunt you in the long run. But if you act like you are being watched or like someone else is going to be able to see these actions, or know about them in the near future, you are more likely to live your life in a much better manner. Yes, you do have a private life, but that does not give you permission to act in hurtful and bad ways when you think that no one else is watching.

Chapter 5: Learn How to Be Virtuous

You have complete control over what is in your mind. You can control the thoughts that go there and you can even find solitude inside of your mind as long as you learn how to get rid of some of the negative thoughts that are in there and make your mind serene. But, you have no control over how others are going to view you. If someone doesn't like you, it is unlikely that you are going to be able to get them to change their minds. This doesn't mean that you shouldn't behave in a manner that is virtuous; in fact, this is a way that you should act even if everyone in the room doesn't like you.

But how does Stoicism see these virtues? Virtues are going to be seen as the moral excellence of the person. They can include traits such as being kind, brave, forgiving, honest, and respectful just to name a few. Since virtues are considered a good and positive trait, the people who are seen as virtuous are ones who will be committed to doing the thing that is right, no matter what it is going to cost them. They are not going to bend into any of their personal urges, desires, or impulses, but they will stick to their own values and their own principles.

Virtues are something that can be taught to children at a young age, but it is important to realize that no one is considered perfect and you are able to cultivate these virtues and make them into new habits for your life. When you work to make virtues into a habit, even if you do fail on occasion, you are taking some control in your own life and you will redirect it towards some happiness and peace.

Regardless of the culture that you are in, virtues are going to be recognized as the basic qualities that are needed for the well-being of the person. They are so necessary because when they are used, they are going to attract the things that are missing from our lives. When you declare that you are going to persevere for these virtues in your life, you are already on the road to success.

We often already know ahead of time what it is going to take to persevere and reach our own personal goals, and yet it is still so hard for us to attain them. We know that if we learn how to forgive someone, it is going to lead us to not be upset or angry with them. But it takes a lot of courage to forgive others and sometimes it is easier for us to just ignore these virtues because it seems easier. But when we learn that the virtues are going to be there to help us succeed and can be a great part of the stoic philosophy, it is easier to pick the right course of action.

There are a lot of examples of when you could use these virtues in order to attain some of your goals and to better yourself as a person. Some of these include:

- Discipline: when you have discipline in your life, it is going to allow you to achieve some of your goals. It is hard to reach some goals such as being a healthier person or running a marathon if you don't have the discipline to keep going with the training.
- Kindness: it is always a virtuous thing to be kind to some of the others in your life. When you add in some kindness to your life, you are able to help someone who is having a bad day and maybe even get them to smile and turn that day around.
- Creativity: this one is going to result in some ideas that will be able to change how others are able to relate to one another, such as what happens with social media.
- Trust: without trust, it is hard to get along with some of the people inside your life. When there is trust, there is

dependability, intimacy, and some more meaningful relationships.

- Gratitude: when you are inside of a situation that is making you feel low, you can use gratitude to help you to see some of the positives in your life and perhaps even learn how to move forward from there.
- Services: in order to feel truly happy, we need to provide some service to others. This is going to be able to change lives, help to create some better neighborhoods, and can make your community stronger.

The biggest issue that you are going to need to consider here is how you are able to become more virtuous in your own life. The good news is that there are so many ways to bring this in, and finding a good role model, someone who you feel embodies a lot of the things that come with being virtuous, and use them to help you to get to your overall goals.

Keep in mind during this phase that there are going to be people who are against you all of the time. But you need to hold your head up high and not let them get the best from you. There are people who have their own insecurities and their own emotions and they are going to let these take over in the long run. You as a Stoic need to be able to stand up against this and try to look at things logically. When you follow some of the steps in this guidebook, as well as learn how to live a virtuous life, you will find that you can see things through that other person's eyes and you won't feel like letting the emotions take over again.

Chapter 6: Be Willing to Contribute to Others

So now we are going to take a look at the idea of contributing willingly to the various things that are in your area. This means that you are going to be willing to help people out without being forced. You will do good work for others, contribute to society, and do some good deeds, without expecting to have some payment or having people thank you for the work all of the time.

Many of us have all the best intentions of helping out others. We may start out the New Year with resolutions of going out and volunteering to help out others. But then we get busy with work, taking care of our kids, working on a business, running errands, or doing a million other things throughout the day. All of us are busy and often those good intentions go away because we decide that we just don't have the time.

The stoicism philosophy is all about being there for others and helping them out. We are not just working on bettering ourselves or concentrating on just ourselves, we are responsible for helping out the community and making our world a much better place. Volunteering and giving of our time and material possession to others can really help to make life more enjoyable.

Many people will say that they don't have time to volunteer, but often this is just a big excuse that we are telling ourselves. Even if we are not able to devote all of our free time to helping out others, it is possible to do some other things that may not take that much time, but can really help out as well. One of the main things that you will be able to do to help out, even if you are really busy, is to donate. There are so many ways that you are able to donate, either your time or some money and supplies, to help out your community.

There are many different ways that you are able to donate in order to help out the others around you. You are not just stuck with donating your time or donating your money, there are other options that will help out as well. Some of the ways that you can donate and follow the ideas of stoicism include:

- Organize a new fundraiser. You can do this for just one day each year, plus a bit of time to get it all organized, and then donate the money or the different products to a cause that you are passionate about. You can do so many different things with this, such as a bicycle race, a charity run, a bake sale, or something else. You are able to add a lot of creativity to what you are doing here to have some fun with picking out the fundraiser that you would like to do.
- Donate some of those reward points on your credit card. Most of the companies that you have a credit card with will allow you to donate your points to a charity if you would like, or you can let someone you know use them to help out as well.
- Most of us have some extra belongings throughout the home. Go through some of these belongings and then sell them on an auction site. You can then donate some of these proceeds to a charity. Depending on the charity that you are using, you are able to donate the items themselves to the charity instead.
- Changing up the way that you search online can make a difference as well. If you use goodsearch.com when you are online, they are going to donate to a charity that you choose. There are also options for donating to charities when you shop on certain sites, such as Amazon.com

- Every time that you have a bit of change that you didn't use, place it inside of a jar. Then when you get to the end of the year, you are able to cash some of the money at your local bank and give that money to charity.
- If you have a professional service, make sure to donate some of the time to those who aren't able to afford the services.

All of these are great ways that you are able to donate some money and resources to help out others, even if you are not able to give a lot of your time because of your busy schedule. All of us get a bit busy and don't have a lot of free time available, but when we learn how to donate our resources, it is easier.

Contributing to others is one of the best things that you are able to do in order to lead the Stoic life. It allows you to give some of yourself, to think of others rather than just worrying about what is going on in your own life, and help out for the great good. Stoicism is not all about just being around for yourself and hoping that others are going to be there to do the work for you, it is about recognizing that we are all in this world together and need to be there to help out. Yes, we are not supposed to let our emotions control us, but this doesn't mean that we can't have emotions and have the want to help out others, and learning how to contribute willingly to others can really help out with this.

There are a lot of options that you are able to use when it comes to working on helping out others. You can do things that you love, such as helping out children or being at the animal shelter, but you need to do something that is going to help you to get the results that you would like for feeling good and bettering your community.

Chapter 7: Avoiding Revenge

If you have been studying stoicism for some time, you are sure to know that emotions are often the enemy. We often become controlled by the emotions that we are feeling because they will make us react in a way that is not right for our overall happiness. When we get upset about how events are not going the way that we want them too, we may get angry and lash out to some of the others who are near us. This is an unhealthy way to take care of our mental health and our relationships.

This is why there is so much time in stoicism that talks about taking things as they come and not focusing on the things that we are not able to control. We need to be the ones in control of what is going on in our lives, not our emotions, and learning how to avoid these is going to make that easier.

Understanding how your emotions and your thoughts are going to influence your own behaviors is going to be really important, especially for those who are dealing with the intense emotions and who are often ruled by the intense feelings that come and get them. If you are able to understand your emotions and you are able to understand the thoughts that are going to come with these emotions, you are better able to develop a way that is good for managing the actions, and therefore gaining the control.

One of the biggest and most dangerous urges that many people will experience is revenge. Revenge is basically a type of retaliations that will inflict injury in return for something that someone else did. You may seek revenge when someone insults you for example.

The struggle that comes with revenge is one that is pretty old. It is a deep instinct that is inside of many people, but it doesn't mean that we need to let it rule us. In the past, it may have been a way for us to survive and stay safe, but now it is often a damaging emotion that is going to make us feel bad and causes undue harm to that other person. However, we need to learn how to get rid of revenge, because it is an emotion that is going to control us, destroying our lives and those of the ones that are involved.

So why do we feel the emotion of revenge? Researchers believe that revenge is like a form of creating our own justice and that the threat of having this revenge can be kind of a form of protection. It can protect you against what others have done with you, but if you let it, it is going to control how you act. Unfortunately, when you perform revenge on one person, they are going to do the same thing back to you, and it becomes a never ending cycle of hurt, power, and anger.

If you want to live a life that is full and is happy, it is time to stop relying on the revenge as the emotion that is going to make you feel better and help you out. There is ample proof that this is just not so, so now it is time to make some changes.

The first thing that you can do in order to stop the revenge is to learn how to be mindful of the feelings that you have. Many times the revenge feelings that you have will be boiled down to some of the basic instincts that we need to survive, but it isn't an excuse for you to act out on those instincts. You need to use mindfulness in order to accept the urges and the thoughts that you have and then learn better ways to avoid these actions.

One of the reasons that we are going to feel like we need to get revenge is because a breach of trust happened. Trust is really important in all relationships, whether it is a close family member or with one of your neighbors and without trust, societies will have a hard time cooperating. When you see someone participating in revenge, it is usually because this trust was broken. Even if it brings you a little bit of satisfaction, it is going to end up adding more problems and suffering in the long run and it is unlikely that you will be able to re-establish that trust as more revenge usually occurs.

The second step that you should work on is to wait before reacting. If you react in anger in the moment, you are going to do something that you regret. But if you wait until you feel a little calmer and the emotions are better in check, it is so much easier to think rationally about your decisions. When you react impulsively on these urges, you are going to let the emotion take over you and you will create a lot of suffering for yourself and for others.

While you are waiting for these emotions to calm down a little bit, you should consider whether your feelings of a loss of trust is actually justified. Are you sure that you have the right information in place about what is really going on or do you need some more information before jumping to conclusions? Even if you find that the other person behaved in a way that may have been hurtful, it is better to find a different path to repair that trust rather than going with revenge.

Getting through this revenge is going to be tough. You want to act on the instincts, but this is you letting the emotions get control over you, and this is not something that is allowed with stoicism. If you are finding it tough to ignore the emotions of revenge, think of the last time that you reacted to these emotions. Was the experience something that you want to repeat? Did you get the results that you were looking for, or did this make things worse?

When we allow our emotions to get the best of us, it is hard to act in a way that loves ourselves or the others around us. We need to learn to find the better path, the path that lets us be in control, and we will see such amazing results in the long run.

Revenge is one of the worst feelings that we can deal with in the long run. It is going to make us feel like we are worthless and that we are not able to take control over our own emotions. There are going to be times when we think it will make us happy, but once the act is done, we are going to feel guilty and like we did something horrible, and it often sets off a chain reaction that just gets worse and worse. Learning how to control those feelings of anger can make a huge difference in how great we feel and how good we are able to feel about ourselves.

Chapter 8: Exercising Patience in All Things

Patience is one of the hardest things for most people to understand, especially in our modern lives. We are used to getting everything that we want, right at this moment, and we can't understand the importance of waiting for things. When people aren't able to keep up with us, we assume that we are so much better than them and that it is time to leave them behind. But there is so much to enjoy with being patient, rather than letting our impatience rule our whole lives.

Nature is going to work such as a wax with lots of transforming over time, and we need to learn how to be patient with how things are going. There are going to be people who will speak badly of you, regardless of how good your actions are, but being tolerant allows you to stay in control of your own actions so that you don't react in a manner that is bad for you. There are always going to be people who are considered evil and who will try to pry away at your patience and your tolerance, but you have the power to remain in control and stay positive, while also ensuring that your reactions to these people match up to what you want.

There are quite a few benefits that you are going to be able to see when you learn how to be a more patient person. First, you are going to notice that your stress levels are going to be reduced. When you are patient with yourself and with others, you don't have to be so hard on life, and your stress will start to go down. You will start to feel happier overall and you can find that your health is so much better than before.

There are going to be times when your patience is tried and you want to just explode, but remember that you are the one who is in control of your emotions, and when you learn how to practice patience, you will be in the best position possible to handle some of the hard situations in life with poise. When all of this comes together, it is going to help you to be happier, have a healthier life, and to even live longer.

In addition to some of the health benefits that you are able to get from exercising patience, you are able to find that your decision making is better when you use patience. When you take the time to be patient, you will be able to take a step back and look at the whole picture, rather than just looking at the small part that is bothering you right now. You can think about the actions that you want to take, thinking about the pros and the cons of all the actions based on the situation that you are in.

When you just react to the situation right away, without thinking it through, you will find that you are more likely to make some huge mistakes in how you are reacting. You may say or do something that really harms others and can be hard to repair. But when you take the time to think about your decisions, you are much less likely to make these big mistakes.

It is going to take some time to learn how to do this, though. We are creatures of habit and we like to get things done right away, rather than waiting around and weighing the options that come our way. It takes some patience and deliberation to get to this point. But it is the building block to compassion, understanding, and developing empathy; since all of these traits are considered stoic, it is important to learn some patience so you can make the best decisions for you.

Once you learn how to be more patient in all of the actions and thoughts that you have, it is going to be an automatic that you are more understanding and compassionate to those who are all around you. People who are more patient are really good at processing the emotions and the events that they are going through, and they are more likely to come up with better methods for overcoming any obstacles that they are facing. They can also feel some more understanding to some others who are around them because they are able to understand why someone would react in a certain way, rather than taking it all to heart.

Finally, you should consider learning some more patience in your daily life because it is going to help you to learn how to appreciate and understand the idea of growing as a person. When you want to grow as a person, it is going to take some time, and this can be frustrating when you want to get things done quickly. But growing as a person can take some time, and it takes some patience, and having this in place will help you to do so much better as a person.

Now that we have taken some time to talk about why patience is so important, it is time to learn how to develop that patience a little bit. This seems like such a simple thing to work on, but it is actually one of the virtues that we talked about before and it can be difficult in some cases. You may feel that you are getting close to mastering it, and then a new situation comes through and you find that it all goes away. You will have to constantly work to keep the patience around you to feel better, but with some more practice, you can make it all happen.

To get started with this, try to make patience your new goal, for just one day. If you try to do it every day, this can quickly become overwhelming, but if you decide to try to add in a lot of patience for just one day, it is a bit easier to focus. So on that first day, put in some of that conscious effort and think about the actions that you are taking. Remember that this is all about mindfulness as well and being in the moment so that you can really think about how to be patient.

When you get to the end of the day, take some time to observe all of the ways that you were able to make some better decisions, how you better understood the situations around you, and how you were able to get along better with some of the people around you thanks to the help of patience. When you wake up the next morning, you are able to do this again. Taking it one day at a time is going to make it so much easier to feel happy and get the patience to become a habit, rather than trying to tackle it all at once.

If you still feel like you are not able to get some of this patience into your day very well, it is time to slow things down. You are most likely someone who is rushing around and who isn't able to slow down their schedule. It is hard to have patience for yourself and for others if you are always in a rush. When you are done with one topic or project, make sure to take a few deep breaths before you even think about moving on to the next action. Before you react to something that you see or hear about, make sure that you take a deep breath and decide if that action is good.

Another option is to try out delayed gratification. When you want to get that second drink, purchase something that isn't needed or get some more dessert, stop and think about it. You probably don't need those things all that badly, and delaying some of that gratification can help you to grow more of the patience.

And of course, always think about what you want to say before you speak. If you just speak from your emotions you are allowing them to control you, something that is not all that stoic. You need to consider the consequences of the words and whether or not they are going to cause harm or a lot of hurt feelings to someone who comes to talk with you. If the words are not kind or are not necessary, just learn how to not say them.

Patience is one of the best things that you can add to your life when you want to become a Stoic, but it is sometimes one of the hardest. You will need to actively bring it into your daily life to see the results, but once it gets there, you are going to be so happy with the results.

Chapter 9: How to be Sincere, Honest, and Moderate

Three other virtues that are important when it comes to being stoic include being honest, moderate, and sincere. If you find that someone tells you that you are not virtuous, you would work to dispel these notions with your sincerity and even to use some of your good humor in order to disarm them. If you are honest, you are able to bring in trust between you and the other person. Let's take a minute to look at some of these, starting with sincerity.

Sincerity

First, we are going to take a look at sincerity. This is a virtue that is going to come right from the heart. What you say and what you do should be the same as what you mean to do and say. You are not being sincere if you tell other people that you like to ride bikes, but you would rather do anything else or you don't even know how to ride a bike. You can't be a sincere person if you spend your time telling someone that they did a good job when you know that they actually did a horrible job. You aren't able to be sincere if you are always making excuses because you would like to get some revenge on them at some point in the future.

In addition, you need to make sure that you are being honest with others and also true to yourself. If you are able to bring both of those into your actions and words, you are being sincere.

To be sincere means that you are going to be genuine. This means that you are going to act the same way that you do alone as you would if you were around other people. This doesn't mean that you should do what you think others want you to do because this is going to mean that you are insincere, but if you wouldn't say something to another person's face, you shouldn't be saying it when they aren't around. You should always act with sincerity, being careful about how you act and what you say no matter who is around you.

Those who are good at adding sincerity to their lives are also the ones who are good at doing help with others without expecting a reward in return. Giving can often be an expression of your sincerity because you are showing an interest in others and a genuine concern for others.

So what are you going to do if there are situations that will require you to tell a little bit of a lie? What happens if you have a friend who did an audition for a play and you feel they didn't do a good job, but you don't want to hurt their feelings. The option here is, to tell the truth. You can change it up a bit and not be completely direct, but they are going to appreciate it more when they know the truth than feeling like they are being lied to.

One thing to remember is that when you are sincere, you are going to expose yourself. You are going to open up to others about how you feel, your aspirations, and even your motives and sometimes this is going to cause others to react in a way that is insincere. It can be a bit of a shock if you are not prepared for this to happen. If you are approached in an insincere manner for how you are acting, make sure that you don't become confrontational. There are often some issues, like anger and insecurity, that are making it so that others are going to have trouble with how you are.

It is sometimes hard to practice sincerity, especially when you are used to so many others being insincere to you, but it is worth it through the long run.

Honesty

You will find that sincerity and honesty will go together. In order to be sincere, you need to be an honest person, but it is possible to work on your honesty in a way that is separate from the sincerity, and when you work on each separately, they are going to work so much better when they are together.

You will find that when most people are confronted with situations where they want to lie, or if they don't want to hurt the feelings of their friends, is to tell a lie. White lies are basically little lies that people will tell their coworkers, family, and friends when they perceive that it will cause less harm to tell the lie compared to telling them the truth. However, you will find that the white lies, even if they are small, are able to damage your sincerity.

It doesn't matter what the white lie is all about, you will be ruining your sincerity. We may perceive them as not being all that big of a diet, or we say them in order to be polite. But even if you just stretch the truth a little bit, you will find that your emotions are going to become more negative, even if you find that the truth will sting you a little bit.

Sometimes we are going to also lie about our plans. This is most often going to happen when we don't want to do something so we will lie about canceling plans with some others. There are often times when we will make plans with someone that we don't really want to do or that we have no intention to really holding onto. We can then make up something that will make sense for why we can't show up and then we get out of the event. Even though we don't want to do the event, if we promised that we would be there, it is going to ruin our sincerity.

If you are someone who has added a lot of these little lies to their life, it is time to make some changes to be a more honest person. This can be really hard. You can learn how to drop all those lies right now and start to tell everyone the truth, but this is often going to cause a lot of issues in the first place. Most of the time, you should start making these admissions a little bit at a time in the future, starting from this minute, to be honest. Admitting the faults that you are dealing with will put you a step closer to handling what is going on and it can help you to turn life around.

The most important thing that you can do at this point is, to be honest about everything and then sincerity is able to follow.

Working on your honesty and your sincerity is important to working on being stoic. These help you to be true to yourself, ensuring that you aren't being controlled by your emotions and that you are able to get through things in a logical and straightforward way. In addition, it is important to take the feelings of other people into account, and when you are honest and sincere, it is easier to do this as well.

Chapter 10: Feel the Joys of Being at Peace with Yourself

The final thought that we are going to explore in this is how to be at peace with yourself. In the final book of Meditations by Marcus Aurelius, it discusses how we are supposed to love ourselves the best, but there are many times when we are going to value the opinion of others more than we value our own opinions. This is a mistake when it comes to stoicism because we need to remember that our destiny is going to be the same as everyone else's and we shouldn't let them decide how we feel or who we are.

This seems pretty simple, but there are many different things that are going to come into play to help us determine if we are at peace with ourselves. Some of these factors are going to include how we are able to perceive ourselves based on what is on the inside as well as how others are going to perceive us. However, you are the only one who will have to answer to yourself when the day is over and if you are not able to stand in the mirror and feel at peace with the person you are, that is when you have failed. It doesn't matter what other people think about you, only what you think of yourself.

The first thing that you are able to do in order to gain peace with yourself is to learn how to raise your own self-esteem. For the most part, if you struggle with your self-esteem, you are going to be more likely to berate yourself and you will allow some of the others around you to bring you down. To learn how to be at peace with yourself, you need to be able to understand what you are worth, based on your own personal beliefs.

Raising your own self-esteem

To form your very own foundation of self-esteem you will need to learn how to accept who you are right now, not think about how you would like to be. There are going to be times when you will criticize yourself and there are times when you will make changes to who you are, such as trying to lose weight, but if you aren't able to live with some of these flaws, you are going to have a lot of issues with feeling good about yourself, even if you are able to reach these ideals later on.

The idea that should be able to accept yourself is starting to gain ground as being a huge contributor to a positive mental state. It is going to help you to empathize better, have a greater understanding of yourself, and will help you to have a lot more peace of mind.

While we know that there are a lot of good benefits about changing your self-esteem and raising it, it can sometimes be hard to turn into someone who likes themselves, rather than being that person who is going to criticize themselves all the time.

The first step here is to confront your downfalls. You shouldn't be afraid to confront these. Your weaknesses are not a bad thing and just because you think about them doesn't mean that you are stuck with a life that is full of hatred for yourself. It is just fine to recognize what kinds of weaknesses that you have so that you are able to move past them and learn how to play to your strengths instead of falling right back to the weaknesses.

The second step is to take some time and enjoy some of the accomplishments that you have in your life. whenever you are able to do something that is good, you should admit that you were successful. It doesn't need to be something that will change the world forever, but something as simple as making a great meal can help you to feel good about your accomplishments. There is nothing wrong with being happy with the life that you have and taking pride in some of your accomplishments, no matter how big or small they are, can help to raise that self-esteem.

Next, you will need to be able to look into the mirror and like what you see there. This one is the hardest for most people because they are going to have some issues with their own body image, but instead of looking into the mirror and seeing all these things that you don't like about yourself, start looking in the mirror and pick out the things that you like. Focus your energy on these things, rather than on all of the bad things that you don't like.

The things that you like in the mirror do not have to be complicated. You can like the way that your hair looks or even the shirt that you are wearing, but make sure that before you head out the door, you pick at least a few items that you like about what you see in the mirror. Even if it ends up just being one thing, it is better than nothing and can help you to feel so much better.

It is also important to understand that no one is going to be perfect. There are times when you are going to feel depressed and you are going to believe that everyone else is doing better than yourself. And there may be some people who are better than you in some ways, but this doesn't make you a bad person or less than any other time. It is time to stop comparing yourself to others in a negative way and just start seeing yourself for the good person that you are.

Most people are not going to reach all the satisfaction with themselves that they would like. But if you can get there most of the way, you are going to feel so much better.

To work with stoicism, you need to be able to have a good self-esteem and be able to believe in yourself. You are going to learn on this adventure that in order to be happy, you need to be able to find it within, rather than from other people or the other events in your life. When you are able to do this, it is easier than ever to feel happiness and to be a Stoic.

Conclusion

Thank for making it through to the end of *Stoicism Mastery: Mastering the Stoic Way of Life*. I hope it was informative and able to provide you with all of the tools you need to achieve your goals.

The next step is to start implementing some of these tips into your personal life. There are so many different things that you are able to do in order to bring some of the ideas of stoicism into your life. Many times we think that this is an ancient philosophy and it is something that is going to be too hard for us to follow in our modern lives. But in reality, it is important to realize that even in our modern lives, we can use stoicism and sometimes during the most chaotic times in our lives, stoicism will be more useful than ever.

This guidebook took some time to discuss stoicism and how you will be able to use it to help you to get the happiness and fulfilled life that you are looking for. When you are ready to find some simple steps that will help you to add some more stoicism to your life, make sure to read through this guidebook and learn how you can get this done, no matter what kind of lifestyle you are currently living.

To your new and virtuous life!

Stoicism

Live a Life of Virtue - Complete Guide on Stoicism

© Copyright 2017 by Ryan James

All rights reserved.

The following Book is reproduced below with the goal of providing information that is as accurate and as reliable as possible. Regardless, purchasing this Book can be seen as consent to the fact that both the publisher and the author of this book are in no way experts on the topics discussed within, and that any recommendations or suggestions made herein are for entertainment purposes only. Professionals should be consulted as needed before undertaking any of the action endorsed herein.

This declaration is deemed fair and valid by both the American Bar Association and the Committee of Publishers Association and is legally binding throughout the United States.

Furthermore, the transmission, duplication or reproduction of any of the following work, including precise information, will be considered an illegal act, irrespective whether it is done electronically or in print. The legality extends to creating a secondary or tertiary copy of the work or a recorded copy and is only allowed with express written consent of the Publisher. All additional rights are reserved.

The information in the following pages is broadly considered to be a truthful and accurate account of facts, and as such any inattention, use or misuse of the information in question by the reader will render any resulting actions solely under their purview. There are no scenarios in which the publisher or the original author of this work can be in any fashion deemed liable for any hardship or damages that may befall them after undertaking information described herein.

Additionally, the information found on the following pages is intended for informational purposes only and should thus be considered, universal. As befitting its nature, the information presented is without assurance regarding its continued validity or interim quality. Trademarks that mentioned are done without written consent and can in no way be considered an endorsement from the trademark holder.

The History of Stoicism

Stoicism emerged in 300 BC during a time of turmoil in Athens following the death of Alexander the Great and the sage Aristotle. The prominent position held by the Greek city-state (polis) in the cultural life of the ancient world passed on to cities such as Alexandria and Rome. The decline of the polis meant that local rule gave way to bigger political units ruled over by distant governors. The certainty of traditional values gave way to more transient principles.

It was against this historical backdrop that Zeno of Citium founded the Stoic school of thought. It derived its name from the "Stoa Pokile", an open market where early followers of Stoicism would meet and teach the new philosophy. Zeno divided philosophy into three "topoi": logic, ethics and physics. The study of ethics is seen as central to the practice of Stoicism and is supported by "physics" and "logic".

Stoics saw the two topoi as fields of inquiry with logic studying how to reason with the world and physics being the study of the world itself. One famous analogy that Stoics used to explain the relationship between the three topoi is that of an egg, with the shell being the Logic, the yolk the Physics and the white the Ethics.

Zeno also established the following basic tenets of Stoic thought:

- Human happiness is the product of living according to nature
- Logic is a tool and not an end in itself
- Physical theory provides the means to determine right actions
- The basis for certain knowledge is perception

- The duty to choose only acts which are in agreement with nature
- True knowledge must always be accompanied by agreement
- Adoption of a cultural outlook that goes beyond narrow loyalties

Zeno drew many of these tenets from earlier schools of thought. From the Milesians, who thought of nature as consisting of entities that could be methodologically observed, he took the concept of the beauty of nature and the adherence to a cosmic order. From the revered philosopher Socrates, he gained a deeper understanding of human nature. Parmenides of Elea preached the importance of reason and thought while Heraclitus of Ephesus has spoken about how divine fire illuminated all things, as well as the constancy of change.

Zeno was succeeded as head of the school by Cleanthes of Assos, who wrote the Hymn to Zeus, which describes the Stoic reverence for the power of universal law and reason and the cosmic order. Cleanthes' successor, Chrysippus of Soli, was the most productive in terms of developing the tenets of Stoicism, in particular developing Zeno's ideas about philosophy and its parts. He established that physics (theology) and logic are necessary as the means to differentiate between good and evil.

Diogenes of Babylon brought Stoicism to Rome in 155 BC, where it eventually became the dominant philosophy. Its popularity can be explained due to the way the philosophy reflected the Romans' worldview, which emphasized virtues, manliness or toughness.

Under the Romans, Stoicism was intended to serve as a way of life and not just be a collection of abstract knowledge. The most prominent of the practitioners of Stoicism was the Emperor Marcus Aurelius, who used the philosophy as a framework to help him deal with the day-to-day difficulties of ruling the empire.

Other prominent Romans who adopted Stoicism include the poet Lucan, the dramatist and statesman Seneca and the philosopher Epictetus. The philosophy also influenced Roman imperial conquest, due to the Stoic concept of "logos," which refers to the meaning or rational order of the universe. Since the universe was created by God to have a rational meaning, everything that happens is part of some greater good.

Romans came to believe that in order to fulfil the greater good, they had to spread the rule of law throughout the world through conquest. Thus, all Romans had to adhere to the values of duty (officium) and respect for authority (pietas), since every function they undertook for the state was meant to fulfil this larger purpose. Fulfilling their duties to the state also meant fulfilling their duty to God.

Cynicism and Stoicism

Cynicism is seen to be one of the major influences on Stoicism. This ethical doctrine that holds that the purpose of life is to live virtuously without property and possessions and rejecting conventional desires for wealth, fame, power and health. However, instead of retreating from the world, as you would expect from living such as life, Cynics chose to flaunt their unconventional beliefs publicly and would be indifferent to any insults that would be hurled their way. In order to maintain their indifference, Cynics underwent constant training of both their mind and their body.

One of the core beliefs of Cynicism is that everyone should share the world and unhappiness comes from false beliefs of what is valuable. They also believed that it was part of their mission to act as moral watchdogs who told people about the error of their ways. In particular, they were critical over displays of greed, which they believed were a major cause of unhappiness.

While they had no official doctrines, there are a number of fundamental principles that all Cynics subscribed to.

- The goal of life is happiness, which can be achieved only by living in harmony with nature.
- To become happy, one must be self-sufficient and master their mental attitude
- Self-sufficiency is achieved by living a virtuous life.
- Virtue is achieved by freeing oneself from power, fame and other influences that are valueless in nature.
- Suffering is the result of subscribing to false judgments of what is valuable, which cause viciousness of character and negative emotions

Stoicism subscribed to the basic principles of Cynicism, but sought to tone down some of their more extreme beliefs in order to make following the belief system easier. For instance, while Stoics believed in living life in accordance with nature, they believed in understanding natural laws so they can consciously follow them rather than trying to overcome them.

Another difference between Stoics and Cynics is that Stoics don't want to change the world, unlike Cynics who are trying to change people's attitudes by acting as moral watchdogs. Instead, Stoics cultivate an attitude of passive detachment, not allowing anything in the world to affect them emotionally and not judging anything as good or bad. The Stoic simply accepts what is and instead of trying to change external events, controls their mental state.

Stoics also emphasize the value of rationality. By being rational, we are able to understand that whatever is going to happen will happen (a doctrine known as determinism, which believes that everything that happens in the external world has a cause, but not everything that happens in the mental world does; thus the only control we can exert is over our mental events).

In order to avoid the loss of personal freedom, Stoics avoid identifying with anything in the external world, such as their job, their possessions or even there loved ones. For example, they would avoid identifying themselves as the owner of this house or car, or as the vice president of this company. If their identity is tied to these external things, what happens when they are lost? What is your identify if you are fired from your company or if you lose your house?

Similarly, if we use external success in order to measure our self-worth, we create anxiety. What happens when we fail? This detached attitude does not mean that we cannot enjoy worldly pleasures or material success, but that these things are not part of our authentic, internal selves.

Thus, the Stoic places great emphasis on self-discipline in order to overcome irrational emotions such as pride, anger or guilt. The Greek word for training to overcome these feelings is "apatheia", which is living without feelings that interfere with living virtuously and is different from "apathy" which is a total lack of emotion.

One important technique that Stoics use to control desire is to distinguish between wants and needs. Needs are those that we need to keep us alive, such as food and shelter, while wants are those things that only serve to meet our desires.

Christianity and Stoicism

Since Stoicism was the dominant philosophy in Rome, it should not be surprising that several aspects of it made its way into Christianity. For instance, some scholars see parallels between the Manual of Epictetus and Paul's discussion of nature and how it is taught in 1 Corinthians. Other aspects of Stoic thought, such as the belief in a rational plan for the universe and monotheism, also influenced early Christian theology.

Stoic influence was also seen in the writings in the 4th century of Christian apologist Marcus Minucius Felix and St. Ambrose, which dealt with the relation between the passions and reason. In the 3rd century, the father of Latin Christian literature Quintus Tertullian, also revealed Stoic influences in his writing, such as his theory of the agreement between the human soul and the supernatural.

At the same time, however, the early Church fathers saw Stoicism as a rival, questioning tenets such as a physical God. But these debates ultimately proved to be productive as they ultimately helped to develop the basic tenets of Christianity. For instance, Stoics believe that God created the universe and imposed laws to give it order, but failed to answer the question: why would God do all this? The answer that Christianity came up with was that God is not indifferent to his creation, but in fact takes an active interest in it, at least that part which is perfectible since it reflects his goodness.

Stoicism in Medieval Times

Stoicism declined as Christianity grew in popularity, but the philosophy continued to have an influence on many thinkers during the medieval period. Stoic texts such as Seneca's Letters and Epictetus' Enchiridon continued to be widely read, while philosophers such as Thomas More, St. Augustine, Descartes, Adam Smith, Kant and Rousseau, were directly or indirectly influenced by Stoicism.

During the Renaissance, there was a major revival of Stoic thought which was called "Neostoicism". This was led by the work of humanist Justus Lipsius, whose opus De Constantia pointed out that there are aspects of Stoicism that Christians can draw upon during troubled times although he also carefully pointed out the tenets which are unacceptable to Christianity. Other Neostoics included Spanish author Francisco de Queveda, author and philosopher Michel de Montgaine and churchman Pierre Charron. However, reception to Neostoicism was mixed and there was never enough interest for it to become a full-fledged movement.

The most prominent of the modern philosophers to be influenced by Stoicism was Spinoza, whose conception of the world was seen to be very similar to that of the Stoics. Spinoza's ethics were also seen to be profoundly Stoic. However, there were some marked differences = for instance, Stoics believed that God was finite but eternal while Spinoza thought that God has infinite attributes. He also did not believe that there was an underlying order to the world and that God did not direct the cosmos.

Modern Day Stoicism

The late twentieth century saw a revival of interest in Stoicism, both through translations of classic Stoic texts for modern readers and a modern movement sparked by the philosophy's influence on two popular types of therapy: Logotherapy and Cognitive Behavioral Therapy.

Logotherapy was developed by Viktor Frankl, who was a survivor of the Nazi concentration camps and used his experiences to develop his theories. The basic principle behind Logotherapy is that people are motivated by a search for a purpose in life, and this therapy would help them find that meaning. Frankl's attitudinal values theory reflects Stoic thinking by arguing that if a person is confronted with "limiting factors" in his life, what is important is his attitude towards them, such as the way he accepts them and the courage he displays.

Another tenet that Logotherapy and Stoicism share is the role of the will. People can use their will to transform their circumstances or, if they can't learn to accept them. In addition, many Logotherapy techniques have a strong connection with Stoic spiritual exercises practiced by ancient philosophers, including Socratic dialogue, in which the therapist points out new meanings in specific word patterns used by the client in order to give him insights that can help them heal; Dereflection, in which the attention of a person who is too self-absorbed is deflected towards others in order to help him become whole; and paradoxical intention, in which people use ridicule and humor to help them overcome their phobias and the anxiety associated with them.

Albert Ellis, the founder of Cognitive Behavior Therapy (CBT), openly acknowledged the influence of Stoicism. An early version of CBT, called Rational Emotive Behavioral Therapy, proposed that changing faulty beliefs and thoughts (cognitive restructuring) could relieve emotional and behavioral problems. Ellis cited the Stoic philosopher Epictetus, as his source of inspiration. Epictetus believed that the way we interpret events have more impact on us than the events themselves. Suffering comes when these interpretations fail to be realistic and our expectations are not met.

Three core tenets of CBT – identifying unrealistic thoughts through logical thought; learning to accept our circumstances; and identifying which things we cannot control and which we can – are also tenets of Stoicism. Beck's original list of irrational ways of thinking (cognitive distortions) includes exaggerating perceived weaknesses or threats, jumping to conclusions, all-or-nothing thinking, and overgeneralization.

But Stoicism is a philosophy and not a philosophy, and so many contemporary philosophers have attempted to modernize Stoicism. One of the main aims of these philosophers is to reclaim the ancient meaning of Stoic from its common English meaning, which means a person who faces things with a stiff upper lip.

The most comprehensive attempt to update Stoicism came from William Irvine, who redefined Epictetus' dichotomy of control to a trichotomy, in which there are things which are within our control, others which are not, and some over which we can exert partial control. His example is that of a tennis match, wherein you can influence the outcome through the way you play but that your win is not guaranteed since there are variables that you cannot influence, such as the way the wind is blowing or your opponent's skill. Thus, Irvine said, your goal should be to play the best game that you can, since this is within your control. Whatever the outcome, you should accept it with the best grace that you can.

Lawrence Becker made an even more comprehensive attempt at updating Stoic philosophy to 'New Stoicism'. The three important differences between Ancient Stoicism and the new variety are: Becker interpreted the primacy of virtue as maximizing your agency; he reinterpreted the Stoic dictum "follow nature" to "follow the facts"; he rejects the teleonomic view of the universe adopted by the Stoics since this is no longer supported by our current scientific understanding.

In the 21st century, Stoic thinking manifests on the Internet through blogs such as the University of Exeter's Stoicism Today and the Facebook group Stoicism Group. There are also a number of prominent articles such as Julie Beck's essay on why you should think like a Stoic about death and "How to Be a Stoic" by Massimo Pigliucci, which was published in the New York Times and which the author is developing into a book. There is also an annual "Stoic Week" during which participants attempt to live by Stoic principles and submit data to researchers who will analyse them to determine how these principles can change your quality of life.

Ancient Masters of Stoicism

Although it was Zeno who founded Stoicism, it was those who followed him who were really responsible for developing the philosophy as one that could be applied to daily life. In particular there are three names that continue to come up as the most important Stoic philosophers: Marcus Aurelius, Epictetus and Seneca. In this chapter we will take a brief look at their lives as well as how they applied Stoicism.

Marcus Aurelius

Marcus Aurelius was the last of the "Five Good Emperors" under whom Roman civilization experienced the highest stage of its development. Historians write of him with admiration due to his refusal to be corrupted by the absolute power he wielded as emperor. Noted historian Edward Gibbon wrote that Marcus was guided by virtue and wisdom during his reign. Marcus saw himself above all as a philosopher and he sought to live his life based on Stoic principles. He was not only wise, brave and just but also always acted from a sense of duty. It was during his reign that the empire was beset a series of misfortunes, including the most terrible famine in its history and a deadly plague, as well as threats of invasion by barbarians of the north.

Marcus had been interested in Stoicism from an early age, and was particularly influenced by Epictetus' Discourses. He even thanked his teacher Rusticus in Meditations for introducing him to the text and to Stoicism. The ruling emperor of Rome, Hadrian, took notice of his hard-working and serious nature and eventually made Marcus his heir and the successor to the throne.

He ascended to the throne in 161 AD, initially ruling alongside Lucius Verus but becoming sole emperor in 169 AD. His reign lasted for almost 20 years, and he died in 180 AD.

Marcus' main contribution to the development of Stoicism is his Meditations, which are believed to be his personal notebook in which he wrote from 171-175 AD while on campaign against foreign invaders in central Europe. The book is essentially an attempt by the emperor to incorporate Stoic philosophical theories into his daily life by engaging in a series of philosophical exercises. Statesmen ranging from former president Bill Clinton to Wen Jiabao, the prime minister of China have talked about how they were inspired by the Meditations. In fact, when he was elected as president, it was reported that Clinton reread the Marcus' book every year or so.

One of the main themes of the Meditations is the importance of expanding our point of view beyond the personal. Marcus exhorts himself to expand his point of view from that of an individual to embrace a broader cosmic perspective. By embracing the vastness of the cosmos, he believed we would be able to see how superfluous our troubles really are in the context of infinity and how short the time from birth to death really is.

By embracing this larger perspective, Marcus also hoped to learn to view the cosmos as a single unified being. Under this viewpoint, all things are interconnected and combine to create the same universe. There is one god, one reason and one law.

Other important lessons we can draw from Marcus' Meditations include:

Draw strength from others. Marcus believed that man was a social animal, and thus it was in man's nature to cooperate. Thus, he enjoined us to look at the people around us and gain encouragement from their good qualities or virtues.

Practice the Virtues You Can Demonstrate. Instead of obsessing over which virtues or talents we do not have, we should instead focus on our own potential for virtuous living. Perhaps to give himself encouragement, Marcus asked himself if he was aware of how much he had to offer and not give in to weakness by saying, I can't. He also enjoined himself not to settle for less.

Focus on the Present. While there is value in practicing negative visualization and imagining all the things that can go wrong so that we can prepare mentally for them, if done without discipline, it can cause us to be come paralyzed with fear. Thus, Marcus said that we should remember the past and the future have no power over us. Only the present can affect us, and even these effects can be minimized as long as you can determine its limits. And you should heap shame upon your mind if you feel you cannot hold out against it.

Epictetus

Epictetus rose from the most humble of beginnings to become one of the most influential philosophers of all time. His works the Discourses and the Enchiridon went on to inspire thinkers through the ages, including Marcus Aurelius, whose introduction to Stoicism was by reading Epictetus. Many modern day adherents of Stoicism also credit Epictetus with providing them with an intellectual framework to apply the philosophy to everyday life and even to helping them endure and overcome the worst tribulations.

Epictetus was born a slave in the city of Hierapolis in Phrygia (which is today Pamukkale in Turkey. His master Epaphroditus was himself a former slave of the emperor Nero and had become rich and powerful. Epaphroditus noticed the young Epictetus' intellectual abilities and allowed him to pursue his studies. He studied under the prominent Stoic teacher C. Musonius Rufus and, once he gained his freedom, Epictetus taught what he had learned by setting up his own school. However, he and other philosophers were banished from Rome by the emperor Domitian and Epictetus set up a new school in Nicopolis, Greece. There he taught through lectures as well as the example of his life.

During his lifetime, Epictetus apparently wrote nothing down and the works we have from him today are transcriptions of lectures he gave which were preserved by his student Flavius Arrianus (Arrian). Originally, he edited and collected Epictetus' writings in eight books, of which only four still exist. The Enchiridon is a distillation of Epictetus' thoughts while the Discourses are purportedly transcripts of discussions he had with Epictetus, as well as classes he attended.

What these writings make clear is that Epictetus intended Stoicism to be a way of life and not merely abstract concepts to be studied and thought over. In the Discourses, Epictetus is quoted as saying that philosophy means preparing to face the things that come upon us. The ultimate goal was to gain eudaimonia (a term that translates to 'a flourishing life' or 'happiness').

Since most people did not achieve the state of eudaimonia much of the time, Epictetus saw the role of the teacher as identifying the reasons why this is so and providing solutions to remedy this situation. In fact, Epictetus even described his school as metaphorically being a hospital to which students came to be treated for their ills. These ills are the result of mistaken beliefs about the things that we should truly strive for, and investing our hopes in the wrong things.

Although Epictetus believed the people have the free will to choose, this freedom is curtailed by external forces. Thus, we must understand what is within our power, since if we do not do this, we will forever be subject to disappointment and an unhappy life. Thus, although we have to live our lives as sensibly as possible, there are many things that can happen to affect our lives, for good or bad, which are beyond our control.

However, it is within our power to control our thoughts and emotions. This would enable us to adapt to whatever happens. So how do we remain composed in the face of adversity? Epictetus calls on us to learn to make the right use of impressions.

Doing this is a two-step process: first, you become aware of something, and then second, you make a judgment about it. A non-Stoic, when confronted with a disaster, would automatically be carried away by their emotions. A Stoic, on the other hand, would take a step back and say; let me see what I make of it and what the proper response would be.

To illustrate, let's say you are going to the office and your briefcase pops open, and important papers fly all over the place. The non-Stoic would immediately start to freak out, imagining the worst, such as getting a dressing down from the boss. The Stoic, on the other hand, would remain calm and simply start picking up the papers. He would then go to the boss and explain what happened and, if the boss loses his temper and scolds him, well, that would be the boss's problem.

In order to better appreciate how we should live life as a Stoic, Epictetus offered a series of metaphors. For instance, he compared life to a game of dice. The dice, and the stakes we are playing for have no real value; thus, what is important is how we play the game. He also uses the example of a ball game, where what is important is the skill and good judgment that the player brings to the game, since these are the only guidelines that we can use to determine if we have played well, rather than the outcome of the game. In a similar vein, Epictetus said we should view life as a weaver would. Whatever material is available, the weaver must use and, as much as possible, to make the best cloth that he can of it.

However, Epictetus said we should not trudge through life joylessly. Instead, we should see life as a festival organized by God, which we attend and which allows us to bear whatever hardships confront us with joy, since we have our eye on the bigger spectacle that is unfolding around us. Thus, it is the duty of the Stoic to contribute what he can to the festival by fulfilling our duties to God and living as well as we can.

With regard to our duties to God, Epictetus compared life to being in military service, where it is our responsibility to discharge this service to the highest possible standards. He said that each person's life is like a campaign and we have to do everything to at the bidding of the General, and if possible, trying to figure out his wishes.

Seneca

Seneca faced one of the more interesting dilemmas that a philosopher can confront – namely, how can a well-off man, who wants for nothing materially, be a practicing Stoic? During his lifetime, he amassed a fortune that allowed him to live lavishly. Once, for a banquet he was holding, he ordered 500 citrus wood tables with ivory legs. He was even able to loan forty million sesterces to the British, who had recently become a part of the Roman Empire. Even worse, this fortune came from the crimes of the Emperor Nero, who he served.

Seneca was born to a prominent family; his father Seneca the Elder was a famous teacher of rhetoric in Rome. As a boy, an aunt took him to be educated in Egypt, where he was educated under the Sextii school of philosophy, which combined Stoicism with an ascetic neo-Pythagoreanism.

The following years proved turbulent for Seneca. After a stay in Egypt to recuperate from an illness, he started a career in law and politics when he returned to Rome. He found himself in conflict with two emperors: Caligula, who would have murdered him but was dissuaded by the argument that it would be futile since Seneca would surely have a short life, and Claudius, who banished him to Corsica, where he wrote his treatises collectively known as Consolations.

He was eventually able to return to Rome due to the influence of Claudius' wife, Julia Agrippina. Seneca then married a wealthy woman, became a praetor, and became tutor to the future emperor Nero, who ascended the throne upon the murder of Claudius. When Nero claimed power upon Claudius' death, Seneca wrote the speech that he made to the Praetorian Guard, which promised them huge bonuses if they would be loyal to him.

Unfortunately, Nero proved to be one of the most unstable and murderous Roman emperors, which put Seneca in the uncomfortable position of having to justify his crimes. That he was successfully able to do so would affect his reputation among future historians – how could he stick by this murderer? In fact, many have accused him of being a hypocrite, of advocating one thing in his writings while practicing another.

What makes it seem worse is that he apparently profited from Nero's crimes. Nero poisoned Britannicus, the son of Claudius, because he saw the young man as a threat. This prompted Seneca to write "On Mercy", one of his most famous treatises, which uses Nero as its subject and is also addressed to him. In the essay, Seneca says that he, the philosopher, can't teach the emperor anything about clemency and that his treatise is just a mirror to display the ruler's virtues. When Britannicus' fortune was divided up, Seneca apparently received a share, which made him one of the wealthiest men in Rome.

When Nero plotted to murder his mother Agrippina, since he saw her as a threat, Seneca also had to use his writing to condone the act. He wrote a letter to the Senate, in the emperor's voice, claiming that she had been about to launch a coup against the emperor. Seneca eventually withdrew from public life, devoting himself to philosophical pursuits. In his retirement, he wrote some of his most well regarded treatises. But his enemies denounced him as being part of the plot to murder Nero, and he was ordered to commit suicide, which he did with composure and fortitude.

Not every historian condemns Seneca's acts. Some historians argue that since he was viewed at a force for moral restraint, his continued stay with Nero was an attempt to curtail the worst of the emperor's excesses and prevent worse from happening to Rome, in the process sacrificing his good name. This interpretation is bolstered by the fact that during the first five years of Nero's rule, when Seneca's influence over him was at its height, was a period of relative stability for Rome. It was only after Seneca was lost his influence that Rome endured its "nine terrible years" as Nero continued to build lavish palaces.

One of the main concerns of Seneca was helping people control their emotions. Stoics view emotion as essentially being irrational and against right thinking. Fear and anger, for instance, are emotional states in which you are no longer guided by right reasoning. Emotions arise because people make false judgments about situations that confront them.

To illustrate this theory, let's say your house burns down. You would naturally view this as being bad, and therefore it is appropriate to respond emotionally. Stoics, however, would say that the only virtue is good; thus, losing your house is not bad and thus, you should not respond emotionally. Seneca believed that unless people would learn to let go of their emotions, they would be unable to live happy lives.

However, one of his most popular works is the treatise On a Happy Life, in which he set out seven 'commandments to himself' that can be used as a structure for living a Stoic life. These are:

1. I will look upon comedy or death with the same expression.
2. I will despise riches when I have them as when I don't.
3. I will treat all lands as though they were mine, and my property as though all mankind owned them.
4. I will not hoard my possessions nor will I squander them thoughtlessly.
5. I will do everything because of conscience and not because of public opinion.

6. I will treat my friends and foes alike in a gentle and agreeable manner. I will forgive before I am asked, and will seek to compromise halfway with the wishes of honorable men.

7. I will quit this life when nature demands it or reason calls me to dismiss it, and I call upon everyone to witness that I have lived according to a good conscience and followed good pursuits.

The Re-emergence of Stoicism in Today's World

Why are more and more people expressing an interest in Stoicism, to the point where there is actually a yearly event devoted to learning how to practice its principles in daily life? The short answer is that life is hard, and any philosophy that teaches us how to genuinely deal with that is welcome.

Keep in mind that Stoicism emerged at a time when there was great upheaval in the world. People were no longer certain about their place in the world and the certainty of the polis gave way to corrupt and inefficient rulers. Compare conditions then to what is going on in the world today and it should not be surprising why more people are turning to Stoicism to help them deal with unpredictable times. As Seneca points out, what you need if you want to escape the things that harass you is not to be somewhere else but to be another person.

Stoicism encourages us to see things as they are so that we can honestly learn how to resolve our problems, even if it is only in the way we perceive them. Thus, Stoicism puts itself in opposition to self-help philosophies such as those based on "The Secret", which encourage us not to engage with reality but to instead visualize our wishes in the hope that they would come true.

However, Stoicism does not advocate a retreat into our own world, but engagement with the external world and with other human beings. According to the ancient Stoics, practicing virtue meant serving other people, and encouraged a cosmopolitan worldview in which people saw themselves as citizens of the world who were not defined by class, religion or country.

The Stoics used the concept of oikeosis to define our relationships with others. The term comes from the Greek word for home or family and means viewing something as belonging to you. In other words, as Stoics, we should extend our affinities not just to our families but also to our fellow citizens and, zooming outward, to all peoples. As Marcus Aurelius put it, what happens to you is good for the world, but what happens to a single individual is for the good of others as well.

Thus, as Stoics, we do not only look out for our own good, but for that of others as well. This is particularly important in a globalized world where people have to work together in order to solve some of the most pressing problems. Addressing climate change, for instance, means that nations have to undertake global agreements and treaties.

Agnostics and Atheists

Another answer is that Stoicism provides an alternative belief system to traditional organized religion. Unlike religion, which relies on dogma and revealed knowledge, Stoicism thrives on free inquiry and reason. We must use our reason to guide us towards the truth and help us to understand the nature of reality.

The Stoic's insistence on reason as the guiding law of the universe can be very liberating to formerly religious people who have tried to live their lives based on the strict and often illogical rules of religions such as Christianity or Islam. In fact, this Stoic tenet may have penetrated the public consciousness, which explains the common phrase, "everything happens for a reason".

At the same time, there is room for doubt and uncertainty in Stoicism. You don't need to have all the answers; what is important is that you train yourself to think rationally so that you can do the right thing,

But Stoicism can also be welcoming to Christians because of the Stoic belief in a God who created the universe and directs it with a purpose. Of course, not all Stoics appreciated God in the same way: some worshipped him, such as Cleanthes of Assos, who wrote a "Hymn to Zeus," while others seem to have been more agnostic. Panaetius, the last head of the Athenian Stoic school, reportedly said that discussing the gods has negligible value to the Stoic way of life.

The basic reason for this ambiguity can be traced to the fact that Stoics do not perceive God (Zeus, as the ancient Stoics referred to him) in traditional religious terms but as the personification of nature. Zeno, the founder of Stoicism, was said to have been inspired to become a philosopher by "The Choice of Hercules", an allegorical work by Prodicus. Prodicus reinterpreted the ancient Gods as being personifications of natural phenomena such as the moon, sun and rivers, and this led to accusations of atheism. The philosopher Cicero also accused Persaeus, one of Zeno's most prominent immediate students, of being an atheist, since he also interpreted the gods in the same way.

Ultimately, however, Stoicism is a philosophy that is welcoming to both the religious and the agnostic, since the cardinal human virtue is wisdom and you don't need to believe in God to accept this.

Promoting Gratitude

One of the biggest misconceptions about Stoicism is that it is only about enduring life's hardships. But Stoics also promote the idea that we should enjoy life, no matter what it brings. As Seneca put it, the happy man is content with his lot in life, whatever it is, and is reconciled to his present circumstances.

In order to promote their sense of gratitude, the ancient Stoics used techniques such as engaging with "externals" such as fame, money or even good health, in order to remind themselves that the only important thing is virtue. They would also subject themselves to voluntary discomfort such as giving up something that they craved or taking cold showers, in order to foster a greater appreciation for food or warmth, for instance.

This tenet of Stoicism is becoming very popular in today's self-help movement, where people are encouraged to thank their loved ones for what they've done and to keep gratitude journals where they write down things that they are grateful for. As a way of achieving gratitude, self-help gurus also encourage followers to practice mindfulness through centering exercises and being fully present in the moment.

For the ancient Stoics, practicing mindfulness was very important since it enabled them to become more self-aware and thus, be more in control of their emotions as well as being able to detach and see things in a broader context. As the philosopher Epictetus put it, men are bothered not by circumstances, but by their views of them. Thus, he advised, don't expect things to turn out as you wish, but expect that they will happen as they will, and you will get along well.

There was also a technique that the ancients practiced called the premeditation malorum, where they would visualize the worst that could happen in any situation. This would allow them to prepare to deal with it mentally or, as Seneca put it, minimize our fear of the misfortunes of life and be ready to deal with them.

In fact, preparing for the worse can be seen as a refutation of The Secret and similar positive thinking self-help philosophies. By being ready for the worse that life has to bring, we not only can learn to be content but also develop a strong sense of gratitude for the many good things that life brings us.

The Three Disciplines of Stoicism

Earlier we described how Zeno divided philosophy into three divisions: Ethics, Logic and Physics. Epictetus, who lived four centuries after Zeno, sought to reflect these divisions in lived philosophical practice, and so he divided Stoicism into three disciplines in his Discourses. Marcus Aurelius, who was influenced by Epictetus' teachings on Stoicism, continually referred to these Three Disciplines in his writings.

The Discipline of Desire (Acceptance). This discipline can best be summed up in Epictetus' call (from the Enchiridion) for us to welcome events however they happen and not hope that they will turn out the way they wish. The ultimate goal of this discipline for Stoics is the achievement of the loving acceptance of their fate (amor fati), according to philosopher Pierre Hadot.

However, this does not mean that the Stoic will blindly and passively accept everything that comes his way. Many famous Stoics have also continued to take action in the face of overwhelming odds and seeming futility. Cato of Utica marched the remnants of the Republican Army across African deserts to make a last stand against Julius Caesar, and then when he was defeated, chose to tear out his guts rather than submit to the dictator and be exploited for propaganda purposes.

Another interpretation of this discipline is that we should control what we desire. As Epictetus put it: when I see an anxious man, I wonder what he wants. If he did not desire something that is not within his power, he would not be anxious. Many of the things that we desire, which we believe will make our lives better, are not within our power to acquire.

119

Thus, continuing to lust after them will only make us miserable. Instead, we should place our hopes in our own moral character and strive to be models of excellence to the limits of our capacity.

The Discipline of Action (Philanthropy). This discipline involves how Stoics should interact with the rest of the world. Stoics should seek to live in harmony with the community of mankind, which involves taking action when necessary.

This discipline also points out that the outcomes of our actions are not within our power and so we should not take them into account when we act. The only thing that is within our power is our decision whether or not to act, and in what form that action should take.

A common metaphor Stoics use to explain this tenet is that of an archer at a contest. The archer wants to hit the target on the bull's eye so he will win the contest but this outcome is beyond his control. Thus, the only thing he can do is to prepare for the contest thoroughly so that he can perform at this best. The Stoic archer gauges his success not by whether he hit the target or not but by having shot the arrow to the best of his ability.

Being a Stoic means you must act in the world, but not to create a particular outcome but for the good of their own soul.

Marcus Aurelius identified three clauses that Stoics should always attach to their actions:

That these actions are done with a "reserve clause". This is understood to mean that every action is performed with the caveat "God Willing" since the outcome is ultimately beyond our control. If an obstacle blocks the action that you tried to perform, then the "reserve clause" should remind us not to be unhappy about it but instead try to display some other virtue.

That these actions are for the welfare of all mankind. This clause means that when we act, we should also consider how they would affect others. If the action causes harm to others or is not in accordance with the common welfare, then you should not perform it.

That the actions are in accordance with value. This clause refers to the theory of values of the classical Stoics, who divided things into "good", "evil" and "indifferent". Good reflects virtues such as justice and wisdom, while evil reflects vices like cowardice, ignorance and intemperance. Indifferent refers to things that are neither and are further classified into preferred (health, physical beauty, wealth, good reputation) and rejected (death, illness, ugliness, poverty) and unqualified indifferent (those which do not fall into either category).

The Discipline of Assent (Mindfulness of Judgment). Hadot defined this discipline as living in harmony according to our essential nature, based on truthfulness and reason. Thus, Stoics are concerned with being aware of and evaluating their own value judgments since these form the basis of our actions and emotions. By continuous monitoring, the Stoic is able to detect early warning signs of mistaken judgments that can lead to irrational passions, and from there, into vices.

The ultimate goal for the Stoic of following these three disciplines is to be able to work towards a way of life that is in accordance with nature, and is harmonious and consistent.

Stoicism and Mindfulness

Cultivating a state of mindfulness is one of the fundamentals of applying Stoicism to everyday life. It is defined as a state in which you are actively paying attention to the present moment. If you've ever tried to practice mindfulness for any period of time, then you know how difficult it can be. It is very hard to tame our minds and focus our attention. But the benefits of practicing mindfulness are vast. It allows us not to give in to our emotions, since we can observe them from a distance. Mindfulness also lets us fully enjoy our lives by living in the present. As Marcus Aurelius said, those who do not observe how their minds move must be unhappy.

There are six mental exercises that Stoics have used to develop the self-discipline needed to practice mindfulness:

Reflect in the Morning

Practicing mindfulness in the morning is a great way to be prepared for the rest of the day. Very often, when we start the day we feel stressed because we are getting ready to go to work and we feel rushed, we feel pressured because we are afraid we are going to be late, we are thinking about the traffic and other problems we're going to encounter. If you're a mother, you have to get the children ready to go to school, they have to get dressed and you have to make them breakfast. With all of this facing us, it's no wonder we feel a little crazy.

Marcus Aurelius also suffered from the problem of having to get up in the morning and having to face the day. He was emperor and had an empire to run! So what does he suggest? Tell yourself: I have to go to work. What do I have to complain about if I'm going to do what I was born to do? Of course, he also prepared himself for the difficulties that he would face by reminding himself: today I will be meeting ingratitude, insolence, selfishness, interference and ill-will – all due to the offender's ignorance of good and evil. By doing this, his intention was not to start his day on a sour note, but rather to prepare himself to face things as they were, and not as he wanted them to be.

How can we begin our day on a more positive note? By making time for mindfulness practice. You can do so by setting your alarm clock to wake up thirty minutes earlier, for instance.

What activities can you do to practice mindfulness? The simplest one is to take a short walk around where you live. You don't even need to get out of the house if it's not practical or safe for you to walk outside; you can even just walk around your home. What is important is that while you are walking, you are completely in the moment, actively aware of what you are seeing, feeling and hearing.

You can also keep a mindfulness journal. Don't let the word "journal" intimidate you, since you can choose the form in which it will take. For instance, you can use it to supplement your mindfulness walk by writing down, in as much detail as you can, what you observed while you were walking. Or you can write about a memory from your past, putting down everything that you can remember about it.

Alternately you can just write down 500 words on a topic. It doesn't even have to make sense; what is important is that you just let the words out on the page. The purpose of this exercise is to help you remove blocks to your creativity by writing without prejudging what you're writing. Just write and be in the moment.

Here is a simple writing prompt to help you get started. Start by writing down the words "I feel". Complete the sentence and then continue from there. Let's say you write, "I feel bad". Then you can write about why you feel bad, how you feel about feeling bad, and so on.

You can also integrate mindfulness into your morning routine by doing a chore while being in the present. For instance, let's say you're making coffee. Instead of just doing this task automatically or thoughtlessly, you can do it mindfully. Pick up the jar of coffee and note how it feels in your hand. Note how cool the bottle feels and how the curve of it fits into your hand. Then when you turn the lid to open it, note how much pressure you have to exert and what your hand feels like. Then pick up a spoon and note how that feels in your hand. When you dip the spoon in the jar, note what noise it makes and the slight pressure as the spoon penetrates the coffee granules.

No matter what method of journaling you choose, what is important is that you make it a regular habit. One way that you can do this is to set aside a particular time to do your journaling during which you know you won't be disturbed.

Focus on Your Goals

One of the problems with living in the modern world is that there are so many distractions that it can be hard for us to keep our attention focused on the moment at hand, much less on achieving our goals. For instance, our smartphones are constantly beeping, telling us that there is an SMS that has just come in, or there is a new tweet from someone we are following or a new email has come into our inbox.

In addition, there is the pressure for us to be 'multi-tasking' since otherwise we feel we are not doing enough. These days, young people no longer pay full attention when they are watching TV or a movie since they are constantly looking down at their phones, answering messages or playing games. And of course, there is the natural human instinct to procrastinate. When we have a task that we have to complete, and the deadline is not yet close, there is a tendency for us to put it off until the time that we actually have to finish it.

How can you use mindfulness practice to help you focus and achieve your goals? One obvious way is to cut up your goal into smaller, doable tasks, and then do them one at a time. Instead of allowing yourself to be overwhelmed by how much you have to do, focus on a more achievable task that you have to do.

Another method that you can use to help you achieve goals is to turn them into 'non-goals'. What this basically means is that, instead of making long-term plans to achieve your goal, you instead focus on the present and how to integrate into your daily life small methods of meeting your goal.

To illustrate, let's say you want to eliminate your credit card debt. The traditional ways to do so would include making a budget to control your spending and creating a repayment plan. But these methods are all future-focused and require you to be in a state of unhappiness since you are constantly thinking about how much longer you have to go before you are finally debt-free.

Instead, focus on things that you can do in the present. For instance, you can set up an automated debit at the bank to pay for your outstanding balances. You can cut up your cards and only pay for things with cash. And when you are buying things, be conscious about why you are buying them. For instance, you can ask: do I need this, or do I just want it?

Using this method of achieving your goals helps keep you focused in the present moment instead of constantly thinking about your problem and how it's affecting you.

Accept the Natural Way

One of the painful realities of life is that we will eventually lose everything that we love, including our own lives. Everything passes, and we have to accept it. It is the way of nature, wherein things die and move on.

Obviously, accepting loss is very difficult for most people. In fact, even thinking about losing something they love is sure to make them distraught. This is why Stoics prepare themselves to accept loss.

Epictetus advised Stoics to try this mental exercise: imagine a cup that you like. Now imagine that it breaks. You think to yourself, it's just a cup and I can bear the loss. Apply this exercise to everything else that is meaningful to you – your house, car, loved ones, even your pet.

Epictetus pointed out that most people treat others' losses as part of the natural order and say, it happens. But when it happens to them, then it becomes more difficult to deal with the loss. Loss is the way of nature. By yielding to it, you won't blame nature for what happens, but instead focus on what lies within your power to affect.

One way you can deal with loss is to take the long view. Consider the story of the Daoist philosopher Zhuangzi. After his wife died, a friend visited him and found him singing and going happily about his normal routine. His friend was shocked at the way he was acting, and asked him how he could do such a thing.

Zhuangzi explained that, at first, he was distraught. Then he considered that at the start of the universe, his wife did not exist. But then she was born and she existed for a while. Then things changed and she died. If he were to cry, then it would show that I have not accepted the laws of nature.

Marcus Aurelius also advised Stoics to remember that in the long term, not only will you have forgotten everything, but the world will also move on when you're gone and everyone will forget you. Consider how many people were famous in their time, but have been virtually forgotten today.

Practice Virtue For Its Own Sake

When you consider why people do the right thing, there are two main reasons – because they are afraid of punishment if they fail to do it, and because they are following the rules. But for the Stoics, there is a third way – because we seek to understand virtue and to act according to this understanding. This is known as Virtue Ethics.

When a person practices Virtue Ethics, he acts morally based on his character. Virtues are seen as character traits or things that a person does habitually as opposed to a single action. To illustrate, when we say that a person is honest, it is because he consistently acts with honesty. If he were put in a position where he could steal money, he would not give in to the temptation to do so.

How a person should act in accordance to virtue is determined by practical wisdom. This type of wisdom allows the person who possesses it to identify the right thing to do in any situation. One way to develop practical wisdom is to constantly monitor our thoughts. We must watch out for and stop negative thoughts while cultivating positive thoughts or, as Marcus Aurelius put it, thoughts that would befit a social animal. For example, we should avoid envying other people, or thinking the worst of them. We should also not let what others think determine our actions but instead only act in accordance with what we think is right, even if it opens us to scorn and ridicule.

One mental exercise Stoics can use to create a role model is to imagine various scenarios, and then think about what the ideal person would do. From their actions, you would be able to determine what inner qualities they have so that you can start to emulate them. Christians actually perform a version of this exercise when they try to live according to the motto, "What Would Jesus Do?" and ask themselves this question when confronted with difficult situations.

Michael Tait of the Christian rap trio DC Talk, in explaining how he lived the WWJD slogan, told the story of how he and his friends visited a small community outside of Knoxville, Tennessee. When Tait walked into a small store to buy some necessities, three men spoke to him in a racist manner and one of them even threatened to lynch him. Although he felt humiliated and angry, instead of lashing out at the men, he showed restraint and instead spoke to them calmly about how racism is a thing of the past.

You can also perform this exercise using real-life role models. Make a list of people who have qualities that you would like to emulate. Then imagine how they would behave in various situations. You can also practice the opposite – think about the worst person you can imagine and then imagine what undesirable qualities they have. Then think about how they would behave in particular situations so that you can avoid doing the same thing.

Take an Inner Retreat

Going on the occasional retreat can be a great opportunity to recharge your batteries by taking a break from your daily life. It also gives you the chance to reflect and assess your life and decide if any changes need to be made. Unfortunately, the chance to take an actual retreat is very rarely available to us.

However, you don't need to leave home to take a retreat. You can enjoy a retreat inside your mind, which you can take at any time that is convenient to you. You can also decide on how much time to devote to your self-retreat, which can be as little as five minutes a day.

In fact, Marcus Aurelius calls retreats in which you leave home "unphilosophical" since the best place to retreat into is one's own soul, where you can enjoy greater freedom and peace from care. He also advises that when you do self-retreats you remember basic and concise precepts to remove all distress and send you back to your regular life without discontent.

These precepts can be brief Stoic tenets that you will reflect on such as:

Everything changes and nothing lasts forever

What disturbs you is not events but your opinion of them

Although the best place to do an inner retreat is in a quiet secluded area where you will not be disturbed, you can actually have one anywhere and at any time. If it is not possible for you to find a quiet place, you can even have a self-retreat while riding to work on the bus or train or even while in a room with someone watching TV.

Reflect In the Evening

Before you go to sleep, it would also be very helpful in your development as a stoic to take some time to reflect. Seneca, in his essay On Anger, said that he ends the day by reviewing everything he had said and done, leaving nothing out. If he encounters a flaw or shortcoming, he tells himself, "I pardon you now, but see that you don't do it again!"

Of course, if you've done something good, or have practiced virtue, you should also celebrate it by congratulating yourself. This will help keep your evening reflections positive and not let it devolve to being a blame game. In addition, you should remind yourself of what you had to be grateful for during the day, and give thanks for them.

To help guide you in your evening reflections, here are three questions suggested by Epictetus:

What did you do today?
What did you do wrong?
What did you leave undone?

What is important to keep in mind is that you are not blaming yourself for what happened during the day. Indeed, you should maintain a dispassionate attitude when you are doing your self-review, as if you were watching a movie, not relieving what happened during the day. This will help you keep things in perspective. It might also help if you constantly remind yourself that what has happened is already in the past, and thus, you can no longer do anything about it.

Modern Stoic Masters

There are many people who have successfully applied Stoicism to help them overcome adversity in their lives. In this chapter we are sharing stories of some of these people in the hope that their example will serve to inspire you as well as giving you ideas of how you can apply Stoicism in your own life.

The Stoic Politician

Sam Sullivan used Stoicism to not only overcome horrific physical injury but also eventually get involved politically and become the mayor of Vancouver. When he was nineteen, Sullivan was involved in a skiing accident during which he broke his spine and lost the use of his body. After a six year battle with depression and thoughts of suicide, he used a Stoic approach to disaster to renew his will to live. In the words of Epictetus, Difficulties are things that test men to show what they are.

Epictetus used the metaphor of a wrestling match to demonstrate how we should face adversity. When God matches us with a rough opponent, we should see it as an opportunity to become an Olympic winner, and this cannot be done without effort.

Using these words as inspiration, Sullivan started to take control of his life. He underwent physical therapy to regain use of his interior deltoids and biceps. He asked an engineer to design technology that would allow him to become more independent by doing tasks such as cooking TV dinners and opening curtains.

He also got involved in advocacy for the disabled community, campaigning for improved access in public spaces, services and transport. It was while performing his advocacy that he made the decision to go into public service. In 1993, he won a seat on the Vancouver City Council, running under the Non-Partisan Alliance ticket. He held the position for the next twelve years.

In 2004, when his party was looking for a mayoral candidate, Sullivan drew up a list of possible names. By this time Sullivan was the only member of his party who was still serving on the Council. After all the names on the shortlist said no, Sullivan decided to run himself and won, to his surprise.

Sullivan said that one of the things that drew him to Stoicism was their commitment to public life. At the same time, however, Stoicism also promotes the idea of being detached from worldly values. Thus, you can be a public servant and engage with the world while still being detached from it.

He also pointed out that going into politics was a sacrifice for him due to how depressing it was. In the course of holding public hearings, for instance, he often encountered people who cared more about their personal agenda than the public good. The right response to the toxic environment of politics, according to Sullivan, is not to withdraw but to jump right in. At the same time, he said, you need to maintain a Stoic demeanour in order to avoid getting depressed. Sullivan would try to put things in perspective by pointing out that politics used to be more violent, involving intimidation and violence, but at least in the present day, less blood is spilt.

Sullivan said that he did not go into politics in order to enjoy the "empty praise" of popular opinion, as he put it. Instead, he paraphrased the words of Seneca: it's not how long you remain in office, but what you do while you're in power. In fact, he even admitted being worried when he got high approval ratings in opinion polls, since it may be an indication he was doing something wrong.

Sullivan was mayor until 2008, when he was challenged for the leadership of the party and lost. His rival would go on to lose the election. However, instead of withdrawing from the party, he chose instead to help campaign for the party candidate. Sullivan reasoned that, as long as he was going to leave politics, he wanted to leave behind a gift, which was to provide an example of a Stoic response to adversity. He encouraged his followers not to quit the party but instead try to minimize the damage the leadership fight had caused by sucking up the criticism and move forward.

He added that although he did not use his time in office to endorse or proselytize about Stoicism, he hoped that his actions reflected the tenets of the philosophy, even if he did not directly speak about it. One project that he started during his term in office, however, which he believed did reflect Stoic principles, was the EcoDensity project.

The basic premise of this project is that people will need to live in high-density cities, rather than sprawling suburban communities, in order to make urban living more environmentally sustainable, and sought ways to reduce cities' carbon footprint. Sullivan believes that this project reflects Stoic tenets of living in harmony with nature rather than trying to conquer it.

The Stoic Warrior

James Stockdale has become a role model for those who aspire to practice Stoicism in their daily lives, since he has long been a student of the philosophy and even credits it with helping him to survive his captivity as a prisoner of war in Vietnam.

Stockdale was introduced to Stoicism when he was pursuing graduate studies at Stanford University as a 38-year-old naval pilot. Philip Rhinelander, who was the dean of Humanities and Sciences, introduced him to Epictetus' The Enchiridion, which he believed would interest Stockdale as a military man. Reading Epictetus proved to be a life changing experience for him.

What he learned from Epictetus was the value of disciplined thought. He pointed out that when you discipline your mind, you can't be the victim of anybody, but only of yourself and your failings. Stoics belittle physical harm not because they are not afraid of being hurt but because they are more concerned about the shame they would feel if they failed to do their duty.

His adherence to Stoic principles was put to the test when his plane was shot down over Vietnam in 1965. He was captured by the Vietcong and spent the next seven years in captivity. As his plane was hit and he ejected, his thoughts turned to Epictetus. He started to think about how Stoics would classify things as being either within their power to control and those that are beyond their power. He focused on those things in the first category, since he believed that by coveting those in the second one, he would be dooming himself to anxiety and fear.

As he was being brought to prison, he kept in mind Epictetus' admonition that in order to retain some semblance of freedom, he should wish for nothing and decline nothing since this would make him dependent on others. It is for this same reason that we should never beg because this would result in having to make deals and agreements with his captors.

As he underwent torture and harsh interrogations, Stockdale contemplated the concept of "Stoic Harm", in which physical injury and pain were nothing compared with the shame they would feel if they failed to perform their duty. Or as Epictetus put it, there is no greater harm than destroying the well behaved, trustworthy and self-respecting man inside you.

He determined that he would display no emotion to his captors. As he was marched to daily interrogation sessions he would chant to himself over and over again: control guilt, control fear. He also invented methods of deflecting his gaze whenever he felt that he had lost control under questioning.

As the senior ranking officer among the prisoners, he became their de facto leader. He organized them by developing a tap code so they could communicate amongst themselves without alerting the guards. In order to help them maintain their self-respect, he told them that, while they could not refuse to do every degrading task their jailers ordered them to do, they could pick the things they absolutely had to refuse to do unless they were tortured again.

In a later conversation with business consultant James C. Collins, Stockdale pointed out that the prisoners who did not make it out of Vietnam were the "optimists" who were always hoping for an early release, and eventually died of a "broken heart" when this did not materialize. He added that you must never confuse the belief that you will eventually prevail with the discipline to confront the horrible reality of your current condition.

Stockdale was released on February 12, 1973. He eventually retired in 1979 as a vice-admiral, although the injuries suffered during his captivity prevented him from resuming active flying status. Following his retirement, he became a fellow of Stanford University's Hoover Institution, where he continued to lecture and write extensively about Epictetus and ancient Stoicism.

The Stoic Athletes

It should not be surprising that Stoicism is proving a perfect fit for athletes; after all, like Stoics, athletes also have to learn to bear hardship and pain during training and on the field without complaint. They also learn to control only what is in their power and let go of the rest. They also have to stay in the moment while they are playing and learn to take things a game at a time.

One of the most successful adherents of Stoicism in the sport is Bill Belichick, head coach of the New England Patriots. Under his tutelage, the Patriots have been to the Super Bowl seven times since 2000 and have won five championships. His well-known mantra is "It is what it is" which reflects his Stoic belief in accepting things as they are

Their adherence to Stoic principles has served them well, particularly during times of adversity. Two weeks before Super Bowl 49, the team was hit by the "deflategate" controversy, in which they were accused of deliberately underinflating balls used when they triumphed against the Indianapolis Colts during the AFC Championship Game.

As a result of the controversy, quarterback Tom Brady was suspended without pay for four games based on his alleged involvement. The team was also fined $1 million and were levied other sanctions, such as having to lose their first round pick in the 2016 draft. There was also a lot of media coverage critical of the team, and there were even calls for the Patriots to be banned from playing the Super Bowl.

Due to the discipline they gained from practicing Stoicism, the Patriots were able to put the controversy behind them and win the championship. Belichick is a strong believer in focusing on the "right here, right now", following Seneca's reminder that true happiness comes from enjoying the present without anxiously worrying about the future and to be satisfied with what we have.

Another Stoic technique that Belichick taught the Patriots was negative visualization. They were able to put this technique to good use during Super Bowl 49, when cornerback Malcolm Butler won the game with a goal line interception of Seattle Seahawks quarterback Russell Wilson. Belichick had asked his team to imagine various losing scenarios so that they could practice reacting to them, and this helped give the Patriots the win.

But Belichick isn't the only believer in Stoicism in the National Football League, since the philosophy has reportedly won adherents at every level of the NFL. NFL executive Michael Lombardi has also shared his belief in Stoicism, which started when his wife gave him a copy of the Meditations of Marcus Aurelius for Christmas. The book inspired him to learn more about Stoicism, as he has not only read the works of Epictetus and Seneca, but also taken the thirty-day Stoic challenge.

As part of his Stoic practice, he has a morning routine that includes reading selected Stoic texts and preparing himself mentally to face the day by reminding himself to be concerned only with the things that are within his control. His favorite Stoic quote is from Seneca: the most powerful man is he who has himself in his own power.

The Stoic Businessmen

Stoicism has gained traction in the offices of Silicon Valley tech firms, as an increasing number of CEOs and other senior executives have said they are fans of the philosophy. According to Ryan Holliday, who has written several books popularizing Stoicism by treating it as a life hack, the philosophy first attracted the attention of tech company execs when angel investor Tim Ferris purchased the rights to turn Holliday's works into audiobooks. He was soon asked to give talks at the offices of Google, as well as having conversations about Stoicism with figures such as GoDaddy CEO Blake Irving, Twitter co-founder Jack Dorsey and Digg co-founder Kevin Rose.

Given their backgrounds, however, it should not be surprising that they view Stoicism in unique ways. For instance, Tim Ferris views Stoicism as an "operating system" to help him make better decisions. According to him, the philosophy allows you to develop a value system that enables you to make better decisions and calculated risks.

Ferris said that Stoicism helps you to value only the most important things that cannot be taken away from you. One exercise that he mentioned is to regularly live in poverty by subsisting only on the most meagre necessities, so that you would be able to ask yourself: is this what I feared so much?

This greatly helped him as an entrepreneur since it not only helped him overcome fear of failure but also to prioritize where he would give his time and his effort.

However, there are other businessmen for whom Stoicism simply helps them personally rather than directly impacting how they do business. Jonathan Newhouse, the CEO of Conde Nast International was introduced to Stoicism when an acquaintance he met at a restaurant mentioned Seneca. This led him to buy a copy of Letters from a Stoic, and he was so enamoured by what he read that he also went on to read the works of Marcus Aurelius and Epictetus. He now takes a Stoic book with him everywhere he goes.

What attracted him to Stoicism was the philosophy's logical approach to life. There are many things that are within our control, such as our thoughts and feelings, and so we should not become attached to the things that are beyond our control.

Although Newhouse admitted that he did not apply Stoic principles to how he ran his business, he said that its most important value to him was helping him deal with disappointment. He cited as an example that it would be easy for him to be disappointed when his grown children did not act as he wished. Stoicism made him realize that you can't control people, and this was liberating for him.

But he did point out that one of the most important lessons that Stoicism teaches about business is that, no matter how hard you work, there are things that are beyond your control that can contribute to your success or failure. Thus, the only important thing is for you to live a life of moral purpose based on Stoic tenets.

Conclusion

Thank you for reading *Stoicism: Live a Life of Virtue –
Complete Guide on Stoicism.* One of my intentions in writing
this book was to make Stoicism accessible to more people who
were interested in the philosophy and wanted to learn more
about how to apply it to their daily lives.

The next step is for you to start applying what you've learned.
You can start by choosing one or more of the exercises that
we've discussed. Stoicism was intended to be a philosophy that
had applications for everyday life, and so this is a good place to
start using stoic principles to achieve your goals.

One of the major misconceptions about stoicism is that it is
about suppressing your emotions. Stoics are frequently
characterized as those people who are always unemotional, no
matter what the situation. Of course, this is farthest from the
truth. Stoics instead choose to control their emotions in order
to better deal with situations that are beyond their control.

To give an extreme example, let's say that your house burns
down. Most people would react by expressing extreme
emotions such as crying or having a breakdown, and that's
understandable. The Stoic, however, chooses not to give in to
his emotions so that he can better handle the situation. Instead
of expressing emotion, he would instead start assessing what
needs to be done, thinking about insurance and where people
who lived in the house would stay and how to get them food
and other necessities.

Of course, there are some people who would say to the Stoic:
aren't you lying to yourself about how dire the situation is? And

the Stoic would reply: I am not. I realize how serious things are, but I have chosen not to react emotionally so that I can do the things that need to be done.

We can see how people have adopted Stoic principles in their daily lives by looking at some of the case studies we have included. For instance, we have looked at how James Stockdale used Stoicism to help him endure physical and psychological torture as a prisoner of war during the Vietnam War. We have also looked at how athletes such as the New England Patriots have successfully used Stoic principles to help them not only win championships but also get through a serious scandal that befell them just before the Super Bowl finals.

To help you better appreciate what Stoicism is really about, we have also talked about the history of Stoicism, as well as telling the stories of some of the early masters who contributed to its development.

I hope that this short guide was helpful and enjoyable for you to read. I encourage you to go back over it often when you are facing difficult situations in your life so that it can give you inspiration as well as providing you with insight on how you should deal with them the Stoic way.

Thank you!

Before you go, I just wanted to say thank you for purchasing my book.

You could have picked from dozens of other books on the same topic but you took a chance and chose this one.

So, a HUGE thanks to you for getting this book and for reading all the way to the end.

Now I wanted to ask you for a small favor. **Could you please take just a few minutes to leave a review for this book?**

This feedback will help me continue to write the type of books that will help you get the results you want. So if you loved it, please let me know! (-:

Printed in the USA
CPSIA information can be obtained
at www.ICGtesting.com
LVHW081455221123
764632LV00006B/49